ROWDY
REVOLUTIONS

HORRIBLE HISTORIES

ROWDY
REVOLUTIONS

Terry Deary

SCHOLASTIC

To Annie Rainsbury, Chepstow Museum, in appreciation

Scholastic Children's Books,
Euston House, 24 Eversholt Street,
London NW1 1DB, UK

A division of Scholastic Ltd
London ~ New York ~ Toronto ~ Sydney ~ Auckland
Mexico City ~ New Delhi ~ Hong Kong

First published in the UK by Scholastic Ltd, 1999
This edition published 2019

Text © Terry Deary, 1999
Illustrations © Philip Reeve, 1999
Cover illustration © Martin Brown, 2011

All rights reserved

ISBN 978 1407 19159 1

Page layout services provided by Quadrum Solutions Ltd, Mumbai, India
Printed and bound in the UK by CPI Mackays

2 4 6 8 10 9 7 5 3 1

The right of Terry Deary and Philip Reeve to be identified as the author and illustrator of this work respectively has been asserted by
them in accordance with the Copyright, Designs and Patents Act, 1988.

CONTENTS

Introduction

History can be horrible. But some bits of history are more horrible than others. And one of the most gruesome, gory and gut-churning bits of history is the history of revolutions and rebellions. What's the difference between a revolution and a rebellion? Glad you asked me that...

Revolution:
The overthrow of a government by the governed

Got that?

So IF I HAMMER OUR HEAD TEACHER WITH A HALF BRICK AND TAKE OVER THE SCHOOL THEN I'VE TAKEN PART IN A 'REVOLUTION'

PLIP PLOF

It can be fun to be a 'revolutionary' and a winner. Make your own school rules and timetable!

REPLACE BORING HISTORY BOOKS WITH HORRIBLE HISTORY LESSONS FOR A START! PASS ME THAT BRICK!

SNATCH

But wait! There's always a danger your struggle will simply be a 'rebellion'...

Rebellion:
Open (and usually unsuccessful) opposition to authority

7

The trouble with being a 'rebel' (and a loser) is you usually get punished. In your case it may be execution through an overdose of school dinners, or something worse.

If you look in history books you'll find there are lots of 'rebellions' but fewer 'revolutions'. That's because the people in power usually win and the rebels usually come to a sticky end.

Of course most school history books don't tell you what went wrong with the failed rebellions. They don't want you to learn from the rebels' mistakes! But this is a *horrible* history book. At last you can learn the terrible truth, the tricks and tactics that work and the foul fate that awaits the failures.

Of course, you would never actually *use* what you learn from this book to lead a revolution against the people in charge of you! Would you?

Awful ancients

Flood is thicker than water

How did we humans get here on Earth? That's a question humans have been asking ever since they invented question marks.

And there have been a few million answers to the question. Many of these answers involve gods making human beings, and the people of ancient Babylon were among the first to come up with stories to explain it.

Now here's the truth: it started with a revolution! This story may look familiar to those of you who have heard the Bible stories...

The Epic of Atra-Hasis
Chapter 1
1 In the beginning were the gods. And the top god was called Enlil. Enlil was a bossy god.

FETCH MY SLIPPERS! IT'S A GODS LIFE!

2 'Ye shall dig in all the fields and build a mansion made of many rooms,' great Enlil spake unto the lesser gods. Enlil was a lazy god.
3 'Why should we do all the work?' the lesser gods they grumbled greatly. For the lesser gods were lazy too. And so there was a revolution, this the first in all the world.
4 Then the laziest god of all, Enki, came up with a bright idea. 'We are gods. Why do we not make a race of beings who shall do all the working for us?'
5 'Good idea, mate,' his fellow gods said. So they created the human race.
6 And these humans slaved and dug upon the Earth and did great works that pleased the gods. But they did not please the top god, Enlil.
7 'These human beings are far too noisy. How they

squabble, how they argue, how they shriek and how they moan. Let's exterminate these human vermin.'

8 So great Enlil sent a plague that made the humans sick and die. But still some humans lived.

9 So great Enlil sent a famine that made the humans starve and die. But still some humans lived.

10 So great Enlil sent a drought that made the humans thirst and die. But still some humans lived.

11 'All right, that's it,' great Enlil said. 'I'll send a flood and let's see who can live beneath a mile of waves. They have no gills, and they're not fish, they'll drown and that will be the end.'

12 But lazy Enki went to Earth and found a human, Atra-Hasis, such a good man who did not deserve to die. 'Build a boat and load your family, and take a pair of every animal here on Earth.'

13 And Atra-Hasis did as he was told. So, when it rained for 40 days (not to mention 40 nights), then Atra-Hasis and his family lived.

14 And when the waters sank back down and Atra-Hasis landed, then the human race was saved.

15 Of course the mighty Enlil he was cross. 'Who dared to tip the wink to Atra-Hasis?'

16 Then the lazy Enki he spake forth. 'We had to do it. We needed someone who could go on making sacrifices.'

17 And Enlil thought and Enlil spake and he said, 'That's good thinking, Enki, son.' And so he let the humans live.

And here we are today to prove it.

Recognize the story? You're Noah good at Bible Studies if you don't!

But it's interesting that the Babylonian story of creation of humans comes about because of a revolution. Gods refusing to do what they are told.

The story may not be true, but it shows that the awful ancients who wrote it knew all about revolutions 4,000 years ago.

Their message is clear – revolutions have *not* been going on for as long as human kind. They've been going on *longer*!

Mesopotamian munchers

Aristotle was a clever ancient Greek (born 385 BC, died 322 BC) who knew all about revolutions. He said, cleverly...

> *Rulers make their peasants poor. The people are so busy working to make a living they haven't time for plotting. Look at the pyramids in Egypt, for example.*

Around 2,350 years later and rulers/bosses/teachers *still* believe in overworking their subjects/workers/pupils to wear them out and stop them making trouble.

In Mesopotamia around 1780 BC the kings of Mari made their workers build a huge palace. It covered the area of seven football pitches and had 300 rooms. While the peasants scraped a living from farming wheat, the kings ate gazelle meat (which was too deer for the peasants), ostrich eggs (an emu-sing meal but think of the giant egg-timer you'd need) and their favourite ... grasshoppers eaten off wooden skewers (that would keep the kings chirpy).

As Aristotle said, the peasants were probably very jealous of the posh people in the palace, but too exhausted to revolt.

11

Yet that hasn't always worked in history, as some miserable ancient monarchs found to their cost.

Shang bang

In 1046 BC the Shang family who ruled China were overthrown by the Zhou people who used to serve them.

If you have a problem today then you can write to a magazine problem page and get some advice. If the Chinese people had been able to write about their suffering under the Shang family, it might have looked like this...

ASK AUNTIE AGATHA

Dear Auntie Agatha,
Last Tuesday the Shang bully boys arrived in the Zhou province and started

collecting victims for the sacrifice tables in Henan Honan, up to the north of the Yellow River. Now, I don't usually mind, but this time they took my little brother, and my mum was really upset. Just the day before she was saying to him, 'You be a good boy or the Shang men will come and get you!' Well, she was only joking of course, wasn't she?

We tried to argue. 'Who are you to take our Zhou children?' we cried.

They just smirked and said, 'It's not *who* are we ... it's Zhou are you!' And off they went. Laughing at their pathetic joke!

They are terrible people. They went to war with us just to have an excuse to make prisoners of us for sacrifice. They say that their dead kings need the sacrifices to keep them happy. Well my mum's not happy, I can tell you. And why can't the dead kings eat rice like the rest of us?

Anyway, we took a day off work to go and see the sacrifices, of course. The Shang priests write questions on tortoise shells then burn them. They say they see the answers in the way the shells crack. They ask about the weather and they even ask their dead kings if it's a good day to go on an elephant hunt.

And my friend says that when one of them dies they kill all their servants and bury them with the priests. The servants don't even get a rest after they're dead. They have to serve the Shangs in the afterlife! That's not fair, is it?

Here we are living in pit-dwellings, breeding children and servants for them to sacrifice, while they live in palaces. What can we do, Agatha?

Yours,
Angry of
Shaanxi

> *Aunt Agatha replies*:
> In a word – rebel! These Shang shenanigans have gone on long enough. Rise up against them. I am with you in spirit though my body will be staying here because I don't want to get hurt!

The last Shang ruler, Di Xin, claimed he was so strong he could slay wild animals with a blow from his fist. But when the Zhou rebels arrived at his palace his guards deserted him and his fists slew no one. He dressed in his finest jewelled robes, set fire to his palace and died in the flames.

The new Zhou rulers weren't as vicious as the Shangs, but they still enjoyed a little human sacrifice from time to time.

King konquerors

For 140 years the Egyptians were ruled by foreigners from Asia, the Hyksos. These Hyksos, known as The Shepherd Kings, weren't nearly as magnificent as the old pharaohs, but they had conquered Egypt because they had three secret weapons...
- war chariots
- bows and arrows
- slings

But by the year 1550 BC, after 140 years, the Egyptians had realized something ... something *you* realized after 140 nanoseconds ... they could copy the Hyksos weapons, turn them on the kings and defeat their foreign rulers.

Which is what they did.

Writing on the wall

The trouble with rebelling against a powerful leader is you may well get beaten. In that case your enemy may show no mercy in dealing with you. You have been warned!

Ashurnasirpal ruled Assyria around 880 BC and faced many revolutions which he crushed ruthlessly. In 879 BC he had a ten-day-long party to celebrate the opening of his new palace in Nimrud and he invited 69,574 people.

Generous Ashurnasirpal? Not really. He wanted the guests to see the strength of his defences. The message was: *don't rebel against me.*

And he put a description on the walls of his palace of what he'd done to other rebels. The message was: *or else!*

This inscription may have put a few thousand off their ten-day dinner…

He forgot to add, 'Have a nice nosh!'

Revolting Romans

First the Romans were revolting – then they were revolted against.

The myths of ancient Rome say Romulus founded the city and became its first king. There were another six kings after him but, in 510 BC, the last king was such a bad boy he was thrown out in a revolution and the nobles ruled Rome. They did this by picking two men each year to be joint rulers – 'consuls'.

'Plebs' (the peasants) had no vote and, of course, women had no vote.

But ... by 494 BC the plebs decided they didn't like being bossed by the posh (known as the 'patricians'). The plebs ganged up and marched on the patricians. By 370 BC (124 years later) they got the right to be 'consuls'. (Some revolutions are very slow.)

In 133 BC a pleb consul, Tiberius Gracchus, argued for more power for the poor people. They marched on the senate. Tiberius was murdered and his body thrown in the river. (Yes, it was Tiberius in the Tiber.) So much for power to the poor!

But as the Romans took over other countries, they found they were being revolted against. They just marched into your country, told you to work for them, fight for them and obey them. No wonder some people got fed up with the Romans and revolted.

Some rebellions against Roman rule were disgustingly dreadful – just the sort of thing you want to read about in a Horrible Histories book...

Spartacus the slave-star

People in power can seem pretty boring. They have all that power but never *do* anything with it except build statues of themselves, get fat at feasts and send you to sleep with speeches.

Rebels, on the other hand, can be pretty exciting ... they go around beating bloodthirsty bullies, escaping from executions, rescuing friends from foul fates before swimming to safety through shark-infested seas. So, when film-makers decided to make a movie about the Romans they didn't make one about soppy Caesar the hero. They chose the story of the super-slave Spartacus, who rebelled against his Roman masters in 73 BC.

Of course, Hollywood turned the story into an epic film starring Kirk Douglas as Spartacus. It was the usual Hollywood nonsense: handsome heroes and vicious villains, glamorous costumes (except in the scenes with naked people in the bath), big buildings and whacking great lies rather than the truth. You could make a film of the Spartacus story if you're really interested. All you need is what the director Stanley Kubrick had…

- $12,000,000 (in 1960. Let's say about $100,000,000 today).
- 10,000 actors (for the battle scenes. The Spanish army provided 8,000 soldiers which helped a lot).
- Three hours and 16 minutes of film (a bit long, and your audience may fall asleep in the middle, but remember this is an 'epic' … a long, boring story).

OR … you could borrow a video camera and do the Horrible Histories version. Cut out all the romantic rubbish and simply present the *truth* about Spartacus. Here it is…

SPARTACUS DID SO WELL THAT HE WAS SENT TO GLADIATOR SCHOOL NEAR NAPLES WHERE HE BECAME A TEACHER - BUT STILL A SLAVE

THAT'S COS I'M A BRUTAL BULGAR. BRILLIANT!

Pointy Bit

Blunt Bit

BUT SPARTACUS WANTED TO GO HOME. HE ARMED HIS PUPILS WITH KNIVES FROM THE KITCHEN AND LED A REBELLION. THEY OVERPOWERED THEIR GUARDS, STOLE THEIR WEAPONS AND ESCAPED. THEY MADE THEIR CAMP IN THE CRATER OF THE VOLCANO MOUNT VESUVIUS!

I'M A BOILED BULGAR. BAKING!

THE ROMAN ARMY THAT CAME TO CAPTURE THEM WAS SMASHED. THE REBEL SLAVES CONTROLLED A HUGE AREA OF LAND. THEN IT WAS TIME FOR SPARTACUS TO HEAD FOR HOME

I LONG FOR MY BROTHER BULGARS 'BYE!

HOME

UNFORTUNATELY THE SLAVES DECIDED THEY DIDN'T WANT TO GO HOME. THEY FORCED SPARTACUS TO TURN BACK AND ATTACK ROME

I'M A BROW-BEATEN BULGAR. IT'S BEASTLY!

ROME

The Spartacus story

Spartacus is still a hero to many people even though he was defeated. Can you sort out the facts from the fiction in the treatment of his story? Answer true or false…

1 Spartacus's story was turned into a ballet before it was made into a film.

2 In 1914 German revolutionaries named their group after Spartacus and overthrew the government.

3 Spartacus's story was turned into a computer game – slaves against the Romans.

4 The film of Spartacus was so popular US President Kennedy went to the première.

5 The writer of Spartacus wrote it in the bath.

6 The film shows Spartacus being crucified, like Christ, even though the real Spartacus almost certainly died in battle.

Answers:

1 True. The ballet 'Spartacus' was performed in 1953 – seven years before the film. It was written by the Russian composer Khachaturian. What would the real Spartacus have thought of it? Seeing himself leaping around a stage in tights?

2 False. German revolutionaries *did* call themselves the Spartacus League … but they *failed*. Important lesson: if you are going to organize a revolutionary group then name yourself after a *successful* rebel, not a *failed* one. The Spartacus League leaders, Rosa Luxemburg and Wilhelm Liebknecht, were killed by the government forces – just like the real Spartacus. The Nazis succeeded where the Spartacus League failed.

3 True. But in the computer game Spartacus nearly always wins! The Romans can only win if they have a lot of luck. Sadly the real Spartacus didn't have a computer because they hadn't been invented. If he had then he could have challenged the Romans to a computerized war and no one would have been cut or crucified.

4 False. The writer of the film script was a real-life rebel and very unpopular. The American veterans (old soldiers) really hated him and tried to get the film banned and had protest rallies outside the cinemas. It would have upset them to see President Kennedy going to support the film-makers. So President Kennedy was sneaked out of a back door of the White House and went to see it anyway. He enjoyed it too.

5 True. The writer was called Dalton Trumbo – someone has to be. He liked to write in the bath with his typewriter on a tray while he smoked cigarettes. WARNING: Do *not* try this at home – the fag ash makes an awful mess in the bath and someone might want to use it after you. Anyway, that was how Dalton wrote. Perhaps he should have written soaps!

6 True. You can imagine what the real Spartacus would have said if he'd been invited to watch the film…

Teutoburger Wald, AD 9

The trouble with General Publius Quintilius Varus was that he was big-headed. You know the sort of person? You can't tell them a *thing*. They think they know it *all*.

Why was such a vain man put in charge of over 10,000 Roman soldiers? Because he was related to the Emperor Augustus, that's why. And Augustus gave Varus a tricky job: to govern the German tribes. But Varus was big-headed, so he thought…

The truth was that tribes like the Cherusci hated the lousy legions. Of course they *pretended* to be friendly. The son of the Cherusci king, Arminius, was just waiting for the right moment to strike…

And this simple plan worked even though Varus had a warning…

So the Romans set off to put down the small rebellion. Varus felt so safe he allowed the Romans to take their wives and children on the march. The forest grew thick – but not so thick as Varus – and the paths grew narrow. Arminius and his 'friendly' Cherusci disappeared into the trees. When they returned they had a huge army of tribesmen.

A thunderstorm turned the tracks into a swamp and the Roman carts were stuck fast. Lightning brought down huge branches and blocked the way. The three Roman legions were trapped. They had to stand there and take the javelins and arrows being shot from the trees. Their shields were soaked and heavy and useless. Varus finally realized his army was going to be wiped out. He wasn't going to let the Germans capture and torture him.

And that's what he did.

But the Roman women and children didn't have swords to fall on. They were captured alive and faced much more grisly deaths. They were sacrificed to the German gods and their intestines were strung from the trees. The next Roman army to arrive was sickened at the sight.

The Romans weren't used to being defeated. Emperor Augustus panicked and lived in fear of the Germans marching into Rome. The worst he got was a grisly present from Arminius … the head of Varus. The big-head had become a dead-head.

Augustus was so upset he refused to cut his hair or shave his beard for months. He wandered around muttering...

Varus! Varus! Give me back my legions!

While Emperor Augustus moaned this over and over again he often bashed his head against the nearest wall.

As he lay dying, five years after Teutoburger Wald, he muttered...

I did quite well, didn't I?

ERR...

The Romans clung on to power for another 500 years, but that first defeat at Teutoburger Wald was a terrible shock.

SEE? WE'VE BEATEN THEM ONCE, WE CAN BEAT THEM AGAIN... AND AGAIN... AND AGAIN...

YEAH! NO MORE LEGIONS IN OUR REGION

NO MORE VARUS TRYING TO SCARE US!

NO MORE ROMANS ER... ER...

Did you know...?
Even before the disaster at Teutoburger Wald, Emperor Augustus was terrified of thunder and lightning. He believed that the best way to protect himself was to wear a coat made from the skins of seals. Amazingly Augustus was *never* struck by lightning ... so this odd protection must have worked!

Crafty Commodus

Commodus was Roman emperor in AD 189 when the people began to revolt because they were starving. (Lots of revolutions start for that reason, you'll find.)

Commodus was a cruel bully who enjoyed the circus – the arena where gladiators and animals fought to their bloody deaths, *not* the circus with clowns and tightrope walkers! In one day, it is said, Commodus killed five hippopotami with his bare hands. That's five unhappy hippo.

When it came to running the country Commodus had the help of a brilliant slave called Cleander. But even Cleander couldn't prevent the shortage of wheat that left the people hungry in the year AD 189.

A mob marched on Commodus's palace. He was doomed! He could fight five hippopotami but hippopotami don't carry swords and spears to fight back (at least not when they're in the circus).

What could Commodus do?

He met the mob and stood alongside the faithful Cleander...

The mob believed the evil emperor, so they grabbed Cleander and hacked off his head. It didn't get the mob any more wheat but they went home happy and Commodus was saved.

But not for long ... by AD 192 Commodus, who was a few brain cells short of being a half-wit, started to think that he was the ancient god Hercules, returned to Earth. He ran the country in his spare time. Most of his hours were spent watching animals and chained men slaughter one another in the arena.

Much of the work of ruling Rome was left to the consuls. Useful men to have around. Yet Commodus decided...

The consuls decided to get him first. They hired an athlete to go into Commodus's bathroom and strangle him. Luckily the athlete succeeded, otherwise he'd have been for the high jump.

Ruthless rulers

The evil empress

One way to change the ruler of a country is simply to assassinate the old leader. That's one way to make sure they don't hang around to make trouble.

Wu-hou was a clever woman. She managed to become empress of China against all the odds. Today she'd have even more trouble with a name like that. Can you imagine the jokes?

But in seventh-century China her biggest problem was being a *woman*, and a lower-class one at that.

If they'd had television in China then her life story would have made an interesting programme...

IN 655 WU-HOU HAD YOUR FIRST WIFE MURDERED AND TOOK HER PLACE. THEN SHE HAD YOUR OLD MINISTERS EXECUTED OR DRIVEN TO SUICIDE

OOO-OOO!

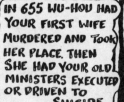

IN 660 YOU HAD A STROKE AND WU-HOU TOOK OVER

FOR YOU!

YOU DIED IN 683 AND THE THRONE WAS TAKEN BY YOUR SON, YOUNG CHUNG-TSUNG!

HELL-OO!

BUT WU-HOU HAD CHUNG-TSUNG PUT OUT OF THE WAY!

BOO HOO!

THE REST OF THE OLD ROYAL FAMILY WERE EXECUTED OR IMPRISONED. YOU EVEN HAD YOUR OWN SONS IMPRISONED WU HOU!

USELESS CREW!

SO, WU-HOU, IN 690 YOU DECLARED YOURSELF EMPRESS, THE ONLY WOMAN EVER TO RULE CHINA!

TRUE

BUT YOUR CRUELLEST ACT WAS TO ARREST A WOMAN WHO LOVED THE SAME MAN AS YOU. WHAT DID YOU TURN HER INTO?

GOO?

NO, YOU SAID YOU'D TURN HER INTO A 'HUMAN SWINE'... YOU HAD HER ARMS AND LEGS CHOPPED OFF!

COO!

BUT IN 705 YOUR MINISTERS REBELLED AND THREW YOU OUT AT THE AGE OF 80!

POOH!

BOOT!

Wu retired to a palace and died peacefully in the year that she was finally overthrown. Did she really deserve such a quiet death after the cruelty of having a woman's arms and legs removed?

Wu-hou united China and many historians think she did a better job than her weak husband and sons could have done. She had one *really* good idea you might like to copy when you take over your country: she said that her Wu family were the royal family – and no one in China with the name Wu had to pay any taxes.

She made a lot of friends that way!

...and Evil Empress II

Constantine VI became the Byzantine Emperor in AD 780 when he was just ten years old. That was the eastern half of the old Roman Empire, so it was a lot of land for a little lad to look after. Sensible Constantine let his mum, Irene, run the country till he was 20.

But on his 20th birthday his mum rebelled and refused to give him his empire back! 'I'm the empress!' she declared.

Constantine was a bit upset, losing an empire like that and his mum breaking her promise. So he rebelled against his rebel mum and had her thrown out. Then the young emperor made a big mistake. A BIG mistake. Two years later, he forgave Irene and let her return!

Would you trust your mum that much?

Was Irene grateful?

Did she behave herself?[1]

Irene not only arranged to have little Constantine arrested. She also had him blinded!

He finally saw what a fool he'd been. (Well, he *didn't* see what a fool he'd been, because he never saw anything ever again, but you know what I mean.)

1 The answers to these questions are 'No!', 'No!' and 'No!'.

Irene only lasted five years before plotters sent her into exile.

Yet this eyeball-mutilating mum is honoured as a *saint* by the Greek Orthodox Church!

What's she the saint of? Opticians?

Singeing scribe

In Basra, Iraq, in 757, a lord rebelled against the ruler of the country, Caliph Al-Mansur. The kindly caliph forgave the lord and ordered Basra's best writer to write out the pardon.

But Basra's best writer was Ibn al-Mukaffa … and Ibn must have been a pea-brained pen-pusher because he wrote a pardon that actually insulted the caliph.

The caliph stopped feeling kind and he did a little writing of his own. He wrote an execution warrant for Ibn al-Mukaffa…

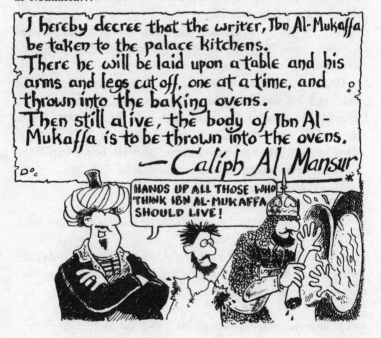

I hereby decree that the writer, Ibn Al-Mukaffa be taken to the palace kitchens.
There he will be laid upon a table and his arms and legs cut off, one at a time, and thrown into the baking ovens.
Then still alive, the body of Ibn Al-Mukaffa is to be thrown into the ovens.
— Caliph Al Mansur

HANDS UP ALL THOSE WHO THINK IBN AL-MUKAFFA SHOULD LIVE!

Miserable Middle Ages

The Roman Empire was so big there were rebellions all over the place. The Roman army held the Empire together, but when Barbarians invaded from outside and rebels fought from inside, the Roman power began to crack.

There had been hundreds of years of Roman historians writing about the horrible happenings. As the Empire fell apart these historians died off and there were few to take their place. So for the next 500 years or so we are a bit in the dark as to exactly what went on. That's why we call those times the 'Dark Ages'. (Not because there was a 500-year-long eclipse of the sun, silly.)

The Middle Ages (around AD 1000 till 1500) started with downtrodden peasants being bullied by barons, crushed by kings and persecuted by princes. It was time to fight back.

In 1307 in Switzerland, the peasants rebelled against their Austrian masters ... that's a *fact*. But *legend* says hero William Tell appeared as their leader. The story goes that he shot an apple off his son's head, was arrested for threatening the governor's life, saved the governor's life on the way to prison, escaped and killed the governor in an ambush.

(So why bother saving him?) But most historians think William Tell, like Robin Hood, never existed. Who can tell?

Tricky Dicky

Rebels who *didn't* kill off the old leader often lived to regret it ... or should that be *died* to regret it?

Little Richard II, King of England, should have died when his peasants revolted against him in 1381. It would have served him right. But the peasants lost because they just weren't organized. Richard had tried to make everyone in England pay a Poll Tax – for the third time in four years. (That's a tax on every 'poll' or 'head' and is not to be confused with the tax pole vaulters have to pay for their equipment.)

Every person in the country (except priests) had to pay four pence tax. If you were a lord with thousands of pounds this was no problem. If you were a peasant struggling to feed your family, then those four pence could make the difference between living and starving to death.

Rebel leader, Wat Tyler, led a march from Kent to London while other rebels marched south from Essex to join him. They were armed with old swords and longbows brought back from the wars in France. On the way they opened prisons, burned down the houses of lords and swore to kill 'all lawyers and servants of the King they could find'.

Sheriffs sweated! Judges were jumpy! Priests panicked! Tax-collectors trembled! Lords looked worried! Bishops blubbered. The peasants were coming to *get* them!

Fourteen-year-old King Richard in London had just 500 soldiers. Wat Tyler's peasant army numbered 20,000. They made their demands...

Deer King Yore Majestie Richud ✷
We the peeple want ~~equallety~~
~~eqwonetree etalaqui~~ to be the same as
wat you is.
- We want **one** bishop. (That's me – John Ball)
- The hedd of the Arch bishop of Canterbry and a few others wat we carn't spel.
- No Poll Tacks not never agen.
- We want to hunt dear in the forest like wat you duz
- Fredom for orl men (but not wimmun)
- We are yore loyle and umble servants

Sinned

X

(Wat Tyler's marc)

That's when the crafty King, tricky Dicky, had a brilliant (but sneaky) idea…

CUNNING PLAN 1
TELL THE PEASANTS YOU'LL GIVE THEM EVERYTHING THEY WANT…

That's what little Dicky did on 14 June 1381. The happy (but gullible) peasants went home. 'We've won!' they cried, as they wiped the blood off their hands.

But some stayed behind. They decided to execute the Archbishop of Canterbury themselves rather than trust King Richard. They grabbed the bish in the Tower of London and chopped off his head. (This probably hurt a bit because it took seven blows of the axe.)

Wat Tyler marched into London and set fire to grand houses. The Savoy Palace was destroyed by gunpowder. But Wat had a strict rule that his followers must not steal from the houses they destroyed. When one of the rebels was found with silver in his pockets he was thrown into the burning palace to die. That's life: one day in Savoy Palace there's the delightful smell of roast pheasant – next day there's the smell of roast peasant.

Still, Wat Tyler was pleased with himself. He asked for another meeting with the King. This time he wanted all the church lands to be given to the peasants.

The King rode out next day and met the rebel group at Smithfield on the edge of London. Again he promised to give the peasants what they wanted. But this time Wat Tyler demanded more and drew a knife which he waved at the King.

Wat a mistake to make!

The mayor of London feared for the King's life, drew his sword and killed Tyler. A few peasants fired arrows at Richard but they were rotten shots and missed. Tricky Dicky rode forward and spoke...

> *I am your captain, I am your King. Quiet yourselves!*

A knight hoisted Wat Tyler's head on the tip of his lance and the peasants saw they were defeated. They laid down their weapons and went home.

FINAL SCORE — RICHARD ONE, PEASANTS NIL!

Did you know…?

Richard II lost his throne to a rebellion 18 years after the Peasants' Revolt. But it wasn't the peasants who finally got him … it was his lords, who hated him just as much.

Not only did the rebels, led by Henry Bolingbroke, throw Tricky Dicky off the throne, but they also made sure he didn't come back by having him murdered. One story said that he was locked in a cell and starved to death. Another story said he was having dinner when seven armed men attacked him with axes.

I KNOW I SAID I'D LIKE CHOPS FOR TEA, BUT THIS IS RIDICULOUS!

Starved or carved? Either way he was just as dead.

Sad shepherds 1

It wasn't very pleasant being a Middle Ages peasant. You were practically a slave to the local lord and had to farm for him and fight for him while he feasted and got fat.

A bit of rebellion and murder would break the boredom. Of course you *hoped* that things would actually *change* by the time your revolution had ended. You *hoped* the fat lord would be finished and you'd be free to live off the fat of the land. Fat chance.

In France there were two revolts by peasants who called themselves 'Pastoureaux' – that's French for shepherds. The first was a failure while the second was a *FAILURE*!

It all started in 1251 when King Louis IX of France was taken prisoner during a crusade against the Muslims in Palestine.

Along came mad-monk Jacob who called himself 'Master of Hungary'. Jacob was a pasty-faced pensioner, who looked like a drainpipe with a beard. Jacob made an astonishing claim…

I HAVE SEEN THE VIRGIN MARY. SHE WAS SURROUNDED BY ANGELS WHEN SHE CAME DOWN TO EARTH AND GAVE ME A LETTER. IT SAYS THE KNIGHTS OF FRANCE HAVE FAILED THEIR KING AND GOD IS ANGRY WITH THEM. MARY WANTS THE SHEPHERDS TO TAKE OVER THE CRUSADE AND ATTACK JERUSALEM!

Why shepherds? Because shepherds had been there when Jesus was born.

Thousands of peasants from the countryside and poor people of the towns dressed up as shepherds and armed themselves with pitchforks and axes. They marched from town to town and frightened the town councils into giving them food and supplies.

Jacob became bolder.

THE CRUSADE HAS FAILED BECAUSE THE CHURCH HAS BECOME EVIL, WHILE I HAVE THE POWER OF CHRIST!

He claimed…

The Shepherds' Crusade

✠ I, Jacob, can heal the sick with my touch, just like Christ.

✠ Food that is given to the Shepherds' Crusade grows more, not less, just like the loaves and fishes.

✠ When we get to the Mediterranean we won't have to sail across it… the waters will just roll back when I command them.

✠ If any of my followers kill a priest then God will pardon them if they drink some wine.

✠ If anyone disagrees with me then he or she will be killed by my bodyguard.

Signed Jacob–Master of Hungary

Clearly Jacob was a few sheep short of a shepherd's pie, but this didn't stop people following him.

The Queen Mother, Blanche, was looking after France while Louis IX was imprisoned. Even she seemed to believe in his crusade and gave Jacob gifts. Meanwhile, his followers went around pulverizing any poor priests they could get their pitchforks into. A boy was hacked to death with an axe just because he was a pupil at a cathedral school.

The march to Jerusalem began, but we'll never know if the Mediterranean would have parted when Jacob ordered it. The shepherds were out of control by the time they reached Bourges. They began to murder and rob the townsfolk – so the townsfolk fought back.

Jacob was hacked to death by mounted soldiers and many of the shepherds were hanged.

WHILE SHEPHERDS WATCHED THEIR FLOCKS BY NIGHT THE BOURGES MEN CAME ROUND AND FASTENED ROPES AROUND THEIR NECKS AND STRUNG THEM OFF THE GROUND

A few Pastoureaux escaped to England where King Henry III planned to capture the new 'Master' who led them. But Henry never had the chance. The savage shepherds were fed up with him and tore their Master to pieces with their bare hands.

RED SKY IN THE MORNING SHEPHERD'S WARNING!

You'd have thought the potty peasants would have learned their lesson, wouldn't you? But did they?

Sad shepherds 2

Seventy years later the shepherds were back. No! Not the same *ones*, stupid. But French peasants with the same *ideas*.

Sadly the shepherds hadn't read their Horrible Histories ('cos most of them couldn't read anyway) and they didn't learn from the first Pastoureaux's pitiful failure.

In 1315, the Pastoureaux revolt started after terrible rains washed out the crops. A potty priest claimed...

THIS IS NOAH'S FLOOD ALL OVER AGAIN! IT'S ALL BECAUSE GOD IS ANGRY! WE NEED TO SEND A CRUSADE OFF TO PALESTINE OR HE'LL BE ANGRIER STILL!

QUACK!

The floods washed away the crops and people were starving. Stories went around that there was cannibalism in France...

The Pastoureaux marched and murdered their way through France on their way to a new crusade. They picked on Jewish families because they believed all Jews were rich and were worth robbing for their money. The *excuse* they gave was that the Jews were murdering Christians by poisoning the village wells and they were drinking the blood of Christian children!

The savage shepherds also massacred colonies of helpless, harmless lepers. The excuse they gave was that the lepers were helping the Jews.

The second Shepherds' Crusade ended like the first one, of course – or should that be 'of corpse' – with crusaders dangling from trees when the army attacked.

Drop-outs

In the 1400s the most unpopular church in Europe was probably the Catholic Church in Bohemia. The Church was rich, the priests were dishonest and mostly foreigners. They were just *asking* to be rebelled against!

Who started the trouble? A teacher. John Hus, who taught at the university, began preaching against the Pope in 1412. He said…

> *The Pope is not the head of the Church … Jesus is the head of the Church! And another thing – a bad pope should be sacked and replaced.*

The Pope, John, wasn't a very happy man and he first banned John Hus from the church ('excommunicated' is the posh word) and then ordered him to appear in front of the Church council.

John Hus wasn't stupid. 'You'll kill me if I appear before your council!' he claimed.

'No I won't!' the Pope replied. 'I'm the Pope. Trust me!'

The Emperor of the Holy Roman Empire encouraged John Hus to meet the council and explain himself. 'I'll make sure you come to no harm!' the Emperor promised.

John Hus went.

The council put him on trial, found him guilty and had

him burned at the stake on 6 July 1415.[1] Which just goes to show ... something.

John Hus's supporters in Bohemia created a new group named after him – the Hussites. Knights and nobles supported the Hussites, King Wenceslas IV of Bohemia gave them power and it looked as if the rebellion against the Church had succeeded.

The ashes of John Hus must have been very happy.

But this was not the 'Good King Wenceslas' you'll have heard about in the Christmas carol. (The 'Good' King Wenceslas was Wenceslas the *first* who was chopped up at a church door by his brother for spreading Christianity through his country.) This Wenceslas IV was weak and was bullied by his brother Sigismund (which is better than being chopped at the church door by your brother).

Sigismund told Wenceslas, 'Get rid of the Hussite councillors!'

Wenceslas the Wimp did as he was told. In July 1419 the Hussites were replaced by new councillors and the Hussite believers were furious. They marched into the town hall, grabbed the new councillors and ... what dreadful death did they have in mind for the enemy councillors?

They threw them out of the window – an upstairs window, naturally.

1 He died singing a hymn. It might have been *Amazing Grace* which he could easily change to *A Blazing Grace* to suit the event.

WARNING: If you plan to overthrow your tyrannous teachers then do NOT throw them out of an upstairs school window! Not under any circumstance whatsoever! You will almost certainly damage the school yard and you wouldn't want that, would you?

Did you know…?

In Poland, in 1410, Duke Witold marched forward to crush forces that were rebelling against him. He gave orders that none of his men was to rob the country they were passing through. Two soldiers were caught robbing a church and their punishment was to build their own gallows and then hang themselves. The men were so scared of their leader that one was heard to nag the other, 'Will you hurry up! We don't want to upset the Duke!' They didn't hang around with building the gallows and they were soon hanging around *from* the gallows!

Sad shepherds 3

By 1419 France had been at war with England for over 80 years and the French were doing badly. The English joined with the French Duke of Burgundy to help him rule the north of France. The French supporters of the rightful prince, Charles, didn't have the heart to rebel … until a girl called Joan stirred them up.

She was a farm girl from the west of France and spent a lot of time in the fields, looking after her father's sheep.

45

It was there she heard voices. Not the usual 'Baa! Baa!' voices, but voices of angels.

The angels told her to lead the French in revolt against the Duke of Burgundy and his English friends. She went off and found Prince Charles and persuaded him to let her try. Amazingly she won battle after battle.

But, finally, the forces of the Duke of Burgundy captured her and handed her over to the English. It's not very sporting to execute an enemy leader just because they fight against you, is it? So the English needed a sneaky plan to get her out of the way.

They accused her of being a witch. They argued, 'Those voices she heard can't have been angels – they must have been devils!'

With a French judge at the trial, the English army and the Duke of Burgundy got what they wanted. Joan was found guilty and burned as a witch … or was she?

That's one of history's great mysteries. There weren't newspapers in Orléans, France, in 1431. But if there had been, the headlines would have been sensational.

Remember, the newspaper is fictional … the facts in the report are incredibly *true*…

ORLÉANS EXPRESS

3 FRANCS   13 JULY 1439

BURNED MAID BACK!

The streets of Orléans were packed yesterday as the whole city turned out to see our heroine, Jeanne the Maid – called by many, Joan of Arc. Pie sellers mingled with pickpockets and priests on a great party day as the Maid rode in an open carriage to the Town Hall.

She wore her famous soldier's uniform of a grey tunic over black leggings and carried the great banner she carried into battle against the evil English ten years ago. Back in 1429, the city was ready to surrender to the English when this gallant girl from Domremy rode into town and stirred the Orléans people into a patriotic passion. Not only did she save Orléans but went on to save France and have our Prince Charles crowned King Charles VII.

Sadly, the English allies in Burgundy captured our Joan and sold her to the English.

After a totally unfair trial they burned her in the marketplace. The cruel enemy built the stake high so the huge crowds could see her. They shaved her head and put her in a simple white dress. Her only cross was made of twigs bound together by a soldier. The fire swept up to her and the last thing she said was 'Jesus!' There is a story that when the English swept up the ashes they found that her heart was whole and wouldn't burn.

Then, just two years ago, the miraculous Maid appeared in Orléans with her brother. No, she hadn't risen from the dead and she wasn't a ghost, she explained. The English had simply switched another witch for Joan at the last moment and set the heroine of Orléans free. On that last visit the city council gave her a few francs and she promised to return. Now she's back and she's been showered with a fortune and feasted at the town hall.

King Charles VII wants to meet his old friend the Maid, the woman who put him back where he belongs. Your reporter went to her inn to interview her about her incredible story. But, this morning, Joan and her brother seem to have left the city and no one is quite sure of her whereabouts.

How did a dead woman appear in front of the crowds? The clues are in the last two paragraphs. But they're not the clues you may think.

Some serious historians have said that…

a) The English made a deal with Joan. They would not burn her if she promised to slip away quietly and lead no more revolts against them. Joan was switched just before the planned execution and she lived.

b) Joan was actually the secret sister of Prince Charles and not a simple peasant girl. When the English discovered who she was they agreed to let her go.

c) The real Joan of Arc turned up in Orléans, where she was a heroine, because she couldn't help going back to see her old friends. Her appearance in Orléans in 1436 and 1439 *proved* that she survived the burning.

Which just goes to prove, some serious historians are serious liars and serious idiots.

There is no doubt that Joan's brother, Jacquemin, appeared in Orléans after her execution and took with him a woman claiming to be Joan. But the clues are 'fortune' and 'disappeared'.

When Joan was alive, Jacquemin acted as her bodyguard and made a *fortune* when she was winning. Once she died he lost his income. So he dressed up a girl *who looked like Joan* and paraded her in front of her admirers. They gave him a *fortune* in money.

Charles VII would not have been fooled by this fake Joan. So, as soon as he heard of her appearance he sent for her. This Joan mysteriously 'disappeared'.

But there is another piece of history that the daft historians ignore. An old history book records...

> KING CHARLES VII ORDERED THIS JOAN TO HAVE DINNER WITH HIM. SHE FAILED TO APPEAR. LATER SHE WAS ARRESTED IN PARIS AND CONFESSED THAT SHE WAS NOT JOAN OF ARC...

No mystery, just a fraud. So, you see, dead rebels don't rise from the ashes ... only cheating historians make them appear to do that.

There is a *small* mystery. Who was this woman who pretended to be Joan and fooled the people of Orléans? There is just a chance that it could have been Joan's younger sister, Catherine.

That's a mystery that may never be solved now.

The real Count Dracula

Count Dracula is a character in dozens of horror films and stories. But there really was a man called Dracula who lived in Transylvania over 500 years ago.

Count Dracula had been a successful rebel and reclaimed his homeland of Wallachia from the Hungarians. But he turned against his old friends, the Turks, and attacked them with horrible cruelty. He made children eat their roasted mothers. When a Turkish messenger refused to remove his turban, Dracula had it nailed to his head. In 1477 the angry Turks were avenged and Dracula was exiled and died.

Pester your parents with this quick question. (The punishment for getting it wrong is to have their neck bitten by your pet vampire bat. Every reader of Horrible Histories should have at least two.)

Question: Prince Vlad of Transylvania had a lot of sick people in his country. They had deadly diseases like leprosy or plague. They were too sick to fight, yet Vlad could still use them in his country's revolt against the Turkish invaders. What use was a seriously sick person in the struggle against Turkey?

Answer: The lepers and plague victims were dressed as Turks and sent to live in the Turkish army camps. The Turks would then catch the diseases and die. A sick Transylvanian just had to return to Prince Vlad with the turban of a dead Turk and he'd get a rich reward. The trick was then to live long enough to enjoy it!

Foul fillings

Christopher Columbus 'discovered' America and its wealth in 1492. (Of course the people who were already there would have said it didn't need discovering.) Within a few years the Spanish were swarming all over South America, terrorizing the tribes and grabbing their gold. The tribes had spears, bows and blowpipes – the Spanish had pistols, cannon and armour. No contest.

Of course the tribespeople often *tried* to rebel against the Spanish *conquistadors*. But only one tribe ever succeeded … the Jivaro.

The Jivaro were tough. A tribesman believed that the only way he could stay alive was by taking the life of another Jivaro. Then, to stop their victim's spirit taking revenge, the victim's head had to be shrunk in hot sand.

The killer would hold up the shrunken head at a feast and the strength of the victim would flow through him.

AND HERE'S ONE I MADE EARLIER...

A woman who held on to the killer's leg during the ceremony could also share that power.

The shrunken heads could be strung on a rope to make a cheerful sort of necklace. The message was clear: 'You don't mess with a Jivaro.'

The Spanish conquistadors didn't understand messages like that. They used the local Indians as slaves to dig gold for Spain. When Philip III of Spain was crowned, the Spanish governor of the Jivaro told them to work harder.

The Jivaro answer was to rebel. They gathered an army of 20,000 and entered the town of Lograno at midnight. The Spanish governor was hauled out of bed and not even given time to put any clothes on. The attackers took the coronation gold and showed the governor what he could do with it.

First they heated it till it was liquid ... and then they poured the molten gold down his throat.

Rich people today have gold fillings in their teeth. The lucky governor of Lograno had his whole mouth done in one go. And you complain about going to the dentist?

The phantom prince

When revolutions start to go *wrong* rebels sometimes invite the old leaders to come back! The solution to this problem is obvious…

KILL THE OLD LEADER! DEAD LEADERS NEVER COME BACK!

Wrong! Dead leaders *do* come back!

Richard III took the throne of England from twelve-year-old King Edward V. Young Eddie and his nine-year-old brother, Prince Richard, mysteriously 'disappeared' – some people say they were smothered by a mattress in the Tower of London.

Fourteen years later, the dead Prince Richard turned up at the head of an army of 6,000 soldiers and demanded his brother's throne back. How did little Richard rise from the grave? Was he a ghost? Was he a zombie? Had he just been holding his breath for 14 years and pretending to be dead?

No. Prince Richard was a *fraud* – a young man called Perkin Warbeck just *pretending* to be the dead prince. But thousands of people believed him.

SO THE TRICK IS TO KILL THE OLD LEADER AND MAKE SURE EVERYBODY KNOWS WHAT YOU'VE DONE?

Exactly! Richard III himself was overthrown by Henry Tudor. Horrible Henry took the naked body of the dead king to the nearest big town and put it on display…

TELL THE BOYS AND GIRLS THAT YOU REALLY ARE DEAD, RICHIE ME OLD SON!

GOTTLE O'GEER! GOTTLE O'GEER!

This is why executed monarchs like Charles I of England or Louis XVI of France were beheaded in public and had their heads raised clear of the body.

Quick quiz

Puzzle your pals with this quaint question. The punishment for getting it wrong is to sit through an hour's history lesson without falling asleep!

The Taborite rebels in Bohemia believed that the world was going to end soon. (That was in 1420 and they're still waiting.) But they didn't want to miss the end of the world by getting themselves killed in battle before it happened. So they invented a weapon, 500 years ahead of its time, to kill without getting killed. What was this secret weapon?

> *Answer*: A tank! At least it was the same idea as the tanks invented in 1916. The Taborites built huge wagons and covered them with wood, studded with iron. Each 'tank' had a crew of 20, some were armed with small cannon and some with flails. If they met a stronger force they would arrange the tanks into a triangle, put the animals in the centre and link the wagons together with chains. It was almost impossible for the enemy to break through.

They defeated a strong German force using their armoured wagons – and it was the Germans who were defeated by the surprise tank weapon in 1916. If they'd read their Horrible Histories they'd have known about the terrible Taborite weapons and been better prepared!

Savage 16th century

Historians agree that the Middle Ages came to a close at around the end of the 15th century and the 'modern' age began. But as far as struggling against leaders goes the 16th century was as bloody as any other.

In 1487 in Mexico, the Aztecs were conquering tribes in the area and making them pay huge taxes. This made the tribes revolt against the Aztec rulers and that's just what the Aztecs wanted. They had an excuse to attack and take huge numbers of prisoners for sacrifices. The prisoners had their living hearts ripped out. It's said there were 20,000 victims in a single ceremony. It doesn't always pay to revolt!

In Wittenberg, Germany, Martin Luther started a religious revolution in 1517 by nailing a notice on a church door. He was *protesting* against the Catholic Church and his followers were known as *Protest*ants. Religious revolts proved to be just as bloody as any other revolts and millions died horrible deaths.

In England in 1536, Henry VIII decided to make his country Protestant. When the Catholics rebelled in the 'Pilgrimage of Grace', Henry promised them a pardon ... then had them strung up by the neck from their own rooftops. Nice man.

Then, in 1566, Dutch Protestants objected to Spanish Catholic rule and began smashing Catholic churches and statues of saints. (Saint Michael, patron saint of underpants, probably got his knickers in a twist.)

Then in England, in 1568, came...

The Northern Rebellion

QUEEN ELIZABETH I FOLLOWED THE PROTESTANT RELIGION BUT HER DUKES OF NORTHUMBERLAND AND WESTMORLAND WERE CATHOLICS. SO, THE DUKES REBELLED AND TRIED TO PUT THE CATHOLIC MARY QUEEN OF SCOTS UPON THE THRONE

Right? Got that? That's what other history books for young people tell you because it's *simple*. But the truth is *never* simple.

The *truth* is the dukes of Northumberland had been like kings of northern England till Queen Liz's father (Henry VIII) had taken away their power. They wanted that power back. Wouldn't you?

Elizabeth had spies who told her about the Northern Rebellion brewing. She wrote to her lords…

> ## My Lord of Northumberland
>
> I command you to appear before me at—my palace in Richmond.
>
> Elizabeth R

Northumberland feared the cold axe on the back of his neck … you can catch a chill that way and sneeze your head off. He came up with an amazing reply…

> ## Your Majesty
>
> I would dearly love to answer your summons to appear at Richmond Palace. Sadly I am unable to attend as I am too busy at the moment.
>
> Thomas Percy, Duke of Northumberland

So she wrote to Westmorland…

> ## My Lord of Westmorland
>
> Wish you were here – or else!
>
> Elizabeth R

Westmorland came up with a better excuse…

> Your Majesty
>
> I daren't come to London because I have enemies there. I would have to bring an army with me, and you wouldn't like that. Perhaps some other time
>
> Charles Neville Duke of Westmorland

What would *you* do if you were the Queen faced by these naughty northerners? Send an army north to arrest them, of course.

The Queen's army, led by the Earl of Sussex marched up to York … then stopped. After all, they didn't want to get hurt!

The northern dukes marched south towards them. They reached Durham – 75 miles north of their enemies. With no soldiers to attack, the rebels turned on the hated Protestant cathedral at Durham.

If you were a brave Catholic rebel what would you attack in the cathedral?

PICK ANY TWO FROM THE FOLLOWING FIVE TO DESTROY

1 The Protestant tables where services were held

2 The Protestant prayer-books

3 The Protestant priests

PTO →

4 The Protestant people at prayer

Rhubarb Rhubarb Rhubarb Amen

5 The Protestant choirboys singing their hymns

Answers: 1 and 2. Yes, I know you would probably *want* to attack them *all* ... but 3, 4 and 5 all had legs and ran away when they saw you coming. So you smashed the poor, innocent table and trampled the harmless little prayer-book on the floor. But don't worry, little prayer - book and table, you will be avenged. In fact, you could say the tables were turned!

The rebels marched on to Barnard Castle, where the defenders began to desert and join the rebels. Since the gates were barred, the deserters had to jump over the walls. The castle commander, Sir George Bowes, reported...

> We were besieged by the rebels and were short of bread and water. I found people in the castle were in continual mutinies, seeking to betray the castle or leap the walls and run to the rebels. In one day the castle lost 226 soldiers, though 35 of these broke their necks, legs or arms in leaping.

Sir George probably enjoyed writing that last bit! But, in the end, he had to surrender.

The northern rebels now held most of County Durham.

But they hadn't captured the castles at Newcastle, Carlisle or Berwick – where no one jumped over the walls to greet them.

No other northern lords joined them and no army arrived from Catholic friends in Spain. Then Elizabeth's forces began to move north to the attack.

Lord Westmorland and Lord Northumberland did what any sensible rebel would do – they ran away.

The Queen's forces murdered and looted their way north and wiped out any remaining rebel forces. Then they started punishing any rebels they could catch. Of 917 County Durham rebels captured 228 were executed – about one in every three.

There were 19 'gentlemen' among the 917 rebels captured. Here's an interesting thing. How many of the 19 'gentlemen' rebels were executed?

a) None at all
b) Six – the usual one in three
c) All 19

Answer: a) Eleven gentlemen were sent into exile and eight were pardoned. Not one was hanged. This wasn't a peasant revolt – this was a revolt of the lords. When it came to punishments the gentlemen got away with it and the poor suffered.

One of the Queen's spies, Sir Thomas Gargrave, wrote to his master, William Cecil, and said...

Is this fair? No. Are you surprised? No.

Suffering slaves

You may think a revolution is planned to change the old ways and bring in something newer and better...

But many revolutions happen because the rebels want to keep the *old* ways. They are revolting *against* change.

That's what happened in 1553 in Peru...

The Spanish settlers in 16th century Peru loved the natives. Because...

• As the Spanish searched for the legendary El Dorado (the kingdom of gold), the natives carried their heavy loads. They were chained together with iron collars and many died on the journeys through the jungles.

• The native tribes paid the Spanish huge amounts of silver, gold, cloth and corn. Some carried the vast riches 200 miles each year to their Spanish masters. Even pregnant women carried great loads. If they gave birth on the journey then they popped the baby on top of the load and carried on!

• The native people worked in the silver and mercury mines till they dropped. They climbed down leather ladders into the mine, then climbed back up 250 metres with the sacks of ore on their backs. If the leather rungs snapped, they plunged back down the shaft. If they got to the top with less than they should, they were beaten.

Life as a native was *horrible*. An officer from the King of Spain wrote a report for the King…

The natives are the most miserable and wretched of any people on Earth. When they are fit they work without stopping. Even when they are sick they get no rest, so few of the sick ever recover. They eat corn and vegetables but never have meat. At night they sleep on the ground in the clothes they wear by day. They can hardly afford to clothe their children, most of whom are naked. They are deeply depressed by their misery and their slavery. They only ask for their daily bread and cannot even have that.

The King of Spain passed a law…

The native people of Peru are free people and not slaves. They must be well paid for their labour and cannot be forced to work.

Then came a bitter revolution that lasted nine months before it was crushed.

Who rebelled, and why?

The answer is that the Spanish settlers armed themselves and rebelled against their King. They argued...

THESE PEOPLE WERE SLAVES WHEN THE INCAS WERE THEIR LORDS. NOW *WE* ARE THEIR LORDS AND THEY ARE OUR SLAVES. THEY ARE *USED* TO BEING SLAVES. THEY ARE *HAPPY* AS SLAVES. WE WANT THINGS TO STAY THE WAY THEY ARE - THE WAY THINGS HAVE BEEN FOR HUNDREDS OF YEARS! WE REFUSE TO OBEY THE KING'S NEW LAW!

The natives – who had the most to rebel about – didn't have the strength to fight against their lords.

The Spanish settlers lost in the revolution against their King, by the way, but it did the natives no good. Slave work and disease almost wiped them out.

Double Dutch

Two Spaniards met in Flanders in the 1560s. They had come there to fight the Dutch rebels. The two knew each other but it took them a while to work out how. Then they discovered they were in fact brothers who hadn't met for years. They embraced tightly. So tightly that, when the Dutch cannon-ball came along, it took off both of their heads together.

OH BROTHER! OH BOTHER!

Quick quiz

Torment your teacher with this revolting question. The punishment for getting it wrong is to swallow a haggis whole...

Question: The Scottish government was Catholic and used friendly French troops to crush Scottish Protestant rebels. The Scottish Protestants turned to the English Protestants for help. But the English failed to take the port of Leith in 1560. The French tricked an English scout into coming close, unarmed, and killed him. How did they trick the English scout?

Answer: The French soldiers left through a small gate in the town walls, dressed as women. The English scout liked women! The French 'ladies' guided him back into the fort. (Scouts should never go after Guides.) Soon this scout was kissing ... the floor. The French cut off his head. The head was then stuck on a pole and decorated one of the church steeples in the town.

Sad 17th century

In England, the 16th-century rebels failed to overthrow their rulers. But their 17th-century successors succeeded spectacularly!

Yes, all right, Guy Fawkes's plot *was* a bit of a damp squib in 1605 at the start of the Stuart reign, but later Stuart subjects rocketed to success. Not only did they get rid of King Charles I but they got rid of his son, James II, too!

Meanwhile, over in Russia, the peasants started revolting, the nobles revolted, Cossack soldiers revolted and their emperors (*tsars* as they called them) were murdered left, right and centre. This jolly period at the start of the 16th century was called by the Russians 'The Time of Troubles'. If they'd known what was coming in 300 years they'd have probably called it 'The Time of Quite Small Troubles Really.'

What a blow!

Prince Dimitri of Russia was assassinated back in 1591. Everybody knew that. But 14 years later along came a man who said…

I AM DIMITRI, HALF-BROTHER OF IVAN THE TERRIBLE. I DIDN'T DIE IN 1591 AFTER ALL!

And they made him Tsar of Russia … for just one year.

Then the Russian nobles (known as *boyars*) decided to rebel against this false Dimitri. On 19 May 1606 they marched to his palace in Moscow, the Kremlin. He did what any sensible fraud would do.

He panicked.

Dastardly Dimitri decided to depart ... but the boyars were at the doyars – I mean *doors*.

So Dimitri jumped out of the nearest window without even stopping to put on a parachute because they hadn't been invented in 1606.

The jump was no problem. It was the landing that gave Dimitri trouble, because the ground broke his fall – and it also broke both of his legs.

The dead-leg Dimitri was doomed. The battling boyars found the body and burned it to ashes BUT...

The real Dimitri had come back from the dead once. They wanted to make sure this one was finally finished fatally and for ever. So they gathered up his ashes, put them in a cannon and blew them to the winds.

Now you'd imagine this would be an end of it all. But, amazingly, it wasn't. Another false Dimitri came along and said...

He gave the boyars a terrible time and almost got the throne back.

Then in 1610, he was murdered by his allies.

Prince Dimitri is probably the only person in history to have died three times!

A head's tale

James I of England survived the Gunpowder Plot and died naturally. But his son, Charles I, upset his parliament and his Puritans with his Catholic connections and they revolted. The English Civil War ended when Charlie's brain-box bashed the boards of the scaffold.

Any old history book will tell you how Charlie's head was chopped and the leading chopper was Oliver Cromwell. But it takes a very *special* history book to tell you what happened to awful Ollie's head. In life Oliver's head was ugly. He had a huge wart over his left eye and a big red nose – he was given nasty nicknames like 'Copper-nose', 'Ruby-nose' and even 'Nose Almighty'.

Revolutions have a strange way of revolving in a complete circle. The hunter becomes the hunted. The chopper becomes the chopped.

Here's a history of the head of England's number one revolutionary. It's all true, so have the sick bucket handy...

3 September 1658 Oliver dies aged 59. Doctor Bates examines the body and cuts off the head. He says the brain weighs six-and-a-half pounds. If it was that heavy it would have broken Oliver's neck when he nodded his head!

He prepares the body for pickling. A French book of the 17th century describes how to do this...

The head should be sawed in two and the brains put into a vessel with the bowels and the blood.

The empty head is packed with lint cloth and sewn up. The body is wrapped in a green cloth like an Egyptian mummy. But it doesn't work. The burial is delayed while London prepares for a grand funeral and the body starts to go mouldy and very, very smelly.

The council can't put the mouldy body on display so they have dummies made with wooden bodies, wax heads, glass eyes and painted faces.

October 1658 One of the dummies goes on display and the public queue for hours to see it. The real body rots in its coffin and the mush dribbles out through the joins. It smells so awful it is quickly and quietly buried in Westminster Abbey around 26 October.

November 1658 The state funeral is held using one of the dummies propped up in a coach. At £60,000 (worth millions today) it is the world's most expensive funeral ever held for a lump of wood and wax. But tourists from around the world come to see the great event.

May 1659 Oliver's son has taken over as 'protector', but he dies and the new parliament invites Charles II to become king. Doctor Bates is suspected of having poisoned Oliver ... and becomes a hero! But Parliament accuses Cromwell and the king-killers of treason. The punishment is beheading and 11 surviving Puritans are executed. Still it's *Oliver* the people want to see punished.

4 December 1660 Parliament votes to dig up Oliver and drag the body to the scaffold for hanging.

30 January 1661 Twelfth anniversary of Charles I's execution. Oliver's body is hanged from nine am till six pm at Tyburn Gallows, London. At sunset the body is cut down and beheaded. Because he'd been pickled and wrapped it takes eight chops with the axe to remove the head. The head is stuck on a six-metre pole over Westminster Hall.

February 1685 Charles II dies and Oliver's head has survived the Great Plague and the Fire of London. Now the head disappears! One story says it was knocked down by a workman and used by boys as a football till it fell apart and the bits got swept into the Thames! Another story says the pole snapped in the night and a guard, Private Barnes, took it home and hid it in his chimney.

1702 As Private Barnes lies dying, he tells his family where the famous head is hidden. They find it and sell it to a Frenchman, Claudius Dupuis. He has a private museum of stuffed animals, waxworks and shoes (!).

1738 Dupuis dies. And the head disappears till Samuel Russell claims he has it. It goes on display in Butcher's Row. And a jeweller called James Cox buys it in 1787. The head is now missing an ear – a story says Oliver's descendants have stolen it. Cox sells the head to T M Hughes for £230. A 1790 drawing of the head shows it held together with tape because it was falling apart.

1799 Head on display in Bond Street, London. Drunken Samuel Russell comes back to claim his old head and causes such a scene that Hughes sells it to a clergyman, Josiah Henry Wilkinson, in 1814.

1827 Josiah writes a history of the head. He loves it! The skin is like yellow leather now, but the hair and beard are still well preserved. A visitor describes the neck as 'black and worm-eaten'. She goes on to say, 'The nose is flat – as it should be when the body was laid face down to have the head chopped off.' There is a hole in the top where the pole has gone through and the teeth have dropped out. Axe marks can be seen on the neck.

1898 Canon Horace Wilkinson owns the head and in 1935 it is borrowed for examination by two doctors. They decide it really *could* be Oliver's because of the warts and pimples that match his portraits. There is even woodworm in the jaw that has spread from the pole!

MMMM! EVEN TASTIER THAN WOOD!

25 March 1960 The head is given to Oliver's old college, Sidney Sussex in Cambridge, where it is buried. A plaque in the chapel says he is buried near by … but not the exact spot. They don't want it to be stolen again. It's still there today.

Even a successful revolution leader can face a terrible revenge once the revolution is over.

Terrible Titus

The slippery Stuarts, Charles II and James II, were Catholics … but crafty Charlie II said…

Until he was lying on his deathbed. Then he came out with the truth…

Then he died.

Why did the Brits hate the Catholics? Because they believed they were plotting a Catholic take over of the country.

Why did they believe that? Because a man called Titus Oates said so.

Why did the Brits believe Oates? Because they were STUPID!

It's the most horrible fact of history … some people are daft enough to believe anything, some people are daft enough to believe *anyone*. Even Titus Oates. If Oates had a criminal record it would look something like this…

Name: Titus Oates (named after the Roman emperor Titus who built the Colosseum).
Nickname: 'Filthy-mouth'. So-called because his nose ran a lot and the snot dribbled into his mouth.

Appearance: Low forehead, small nose, little piggy eyes, fat, wobbling chin, porky body.
Speech: Squeaky voice and filthy language.
Born: 15 September 1649, Rutland, England. (The year that Charles I was executed for being too Catholic.)

Parents: Father a Protestant preacher. Mother a Protestant housewife. Titus became well known for the way he swore at his mother.
Schools: 1 Merchant Taylor's School. Accused of disgusting behaviour. Expelled. **2** Westminster School. Accused of disgusting behaviour. Expelled.
College: Cambridge University. Accused of cheating a poor tailor out of the money he owed for a coat. Titus swore on the Bible that he'd paid but was in fact telling whopping great lies. Expelled.
Habits: Liked to dress in fine clothes. Liked to get very drunk. Regularly accused of stealing neighbours' pigs and chickens.
Religion: Became a Protestant priest, switched to being a Catholic for a while and then changed back.

Career:

1674 – became a priest in Hastings – sacked for lying.

1676 – became a teacher. Falsely accused a popular teacher of abusing the pupils and had to run away.

1677 – became a sailor but got into trouble and had to run away.

1677 – became a priest to a Catholic family and met Israel Tonge – Catholic-hater. They begin to plot against Catholics.

1678 – went to Catholic colleges in France to spy on them. Expelled.

If this man swore that there was a plot to murder you, would you believe him?

King Charles II was walking in St James's Park in August 1678 when a friend brought a message from Oates and Tonge, 'There are two Catholic gunmen waiting in the park to shoot you! As soon as you are dead the Catholic King Louis XIV of France will invade Britain.'

Charles II was as clever as you and he said, 'Rubbish!' But the King's council met Tonge and Oates who swore the story was true.

Oates even named 90 Catholic priests and dozens of noblemen as plotters. Truthless Tonge and odious Oates had no proof at all, but they did have two pieces of luck. Firstly, they named the King's doctor, Edward Coleman, as a plotter. It was discovered that Coleman really *had* been writing to the French.

Then, a magistrate who was investigating the case went missing. Five days later his battered body was found on Primrose Hill near London. He had been stabbed with his own sword after he'd been beaten to death. Gruesome and sinister. The Catholics got the blame, of course.

Suddenly everyone believed Oates and his Popish plot. Snotty Titus was a national hero – almost any Catholic was a suspect. Londoners went in fear of their lives – they imagined they saw plotters in every shadow...

• Men wore armour when they went out at night.

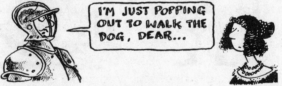

• Ladies carried pistols in their sleeves.

• The cellars of Parliament were searched for another Gunpowder Plot.

- On 5 November the bonfires burned images of the Catholic leader, the Pope.[1]

- Catholic widows married Protestant men to try and show they were loyal.

Titus Oates named five old lords as leaders of a Catholic plot. Charles II laughed – the lords were so old they couldn't lead a Catholic guide dog. But trials went ahead.

1 So that the images would appear to scream as they burned, the image-makers filled the dummies with live cats.

The King's doctor was found guilty and hanged till he was half dead, revived so he could see himself being cut open and his intestines burned on a fire. In all, 35 innocent people died horrible deaths because of Oates's lies.

After two more years of this terror Charles II died. His Catholic brother, James II, came to the throne and it was time for revenge.

Titus was taken to the pillory where he was pelted with eggs and rubbish for two days.

On the third day he was stripped to the waist, tied to the back of a cart and made to walk behind it while he was whipped. Reports say Titus made 'hideous bellowings'. (He was probably trying to say, 'Would someone mind passing me a hankie so I can blow my nose?')

This was repeated the next day when he was dragged on a sledge while he was whipped because he was too weak to walk. He spent three more years in prison before being released when James II fled from England. James's Protestant daughter, Mary, took his throne.

James II, unlike brother Charles II, had at least told the truth and never pretended to be a Protestant. The British people still hated the Catholics and James couldn't last long.

Titus Oates, an outrageous liar and a fraud, had been part of the 'Glorious Revolution' that got rid of Britain's last Catholic king.

Awesome Americans

The British were still troubled by members of the Stuart family who had tried to lead revolutions in 1715 and 1745. They finally saw off the last Stuart rebellion at the battle of Culloden (Scotland) in 1746.

Just when they might have hoped for a little peace and quiet, their colony in a little, far away place started giving them trouble. Of course the Americans argued that the Brits deserved all they got...

Tea is for trouble

By the 1770s the American people were making money in their new country but their British rulers were taking a lot of it in taxes. In return the Brits gave the Americans nothing. The Americans were upset and started making tax attacks.

The rebels were especially upset because the Brits even taxed their cups of tea – three pence to Britain for every pound of tea sold in America.

In 1773, the Americans in Boston tipped the British tea straight from the ships into the harbour.

It was known as the Boston Tea Party and a poem, written at that time, explained the American anger. To understand it you have to remember that Britain is an 'old lady' and America is her 'daughter'.

The Boston Tea Party

There was an old lady lived over the sea,
And she was an island queen;
Her daughter lived off in a new country,
With an ocean of water between.

The old lady's pockets were full of gold,
But never contented was she.
So she called on her daughter to pay her a tax
Of three pence a pound on her tea
Of three pence a pound on her tea.

The tea was conveyed to the daughter's door,
All down the ocean side;
And the bouncing girl poured out every pound
In the dark and boiling tide.

And then she called to the Island Queen,
'Oh Mother, dear Mother,' said she,
'Your tea you may have when it's steeped enough,
But never a tax from me!'

The old lady decided to send in troops to slap the cheeky daughter to teach her a lesson. But the bouncing girl was tougher than she seemed and battered the old lady's soldiers to defeat.

Did you know…?
During the 1777 American Revolution the British were besieged in Saratoga by General Gates's rebel American forces. A British soldier was laid out on a table as doctors prepared to amputate his leg. An American cannon-ball crashed into the room and took off his remaining good leg. His friends ran off … the unfortunate patient was never going to run anywhere ever again.

Bloody battles
First the Americans fought against the British in their War of Independence, then they joined the French to fight the British again during the Napoleonic Wars. When they'd run out of excuses to batter the Brits they fought against themselves in their Civil War. The southern states (the Confederates) revolted against the northern states (the Unionists).

Heroes and chickens
Imagine that you are about to go into an American Civil War battle…

- You will be facing an enemy who would very much like to kill you.
- You are standing on legs that would very much like to run back home.
- You are following orders from a commander who will have you shot if you try to run away. (It's all right for him, of course. He isn't there in the front line with you, getting shot at!)

What sort of soldier would you be? A hero? Or a chicken?

Test yourself with these real Civil War situations. One of the answers is the true one and the other is invented. But which is which?

1 You are Abel Sheeks and join the Confederate army dressed in your blue clothes ... the colour of the enemy! The Confederate army has no spare grey uniform for you. Where can you get a grey uniform from before your own men shoot you by mistake?
a) Save up your pay for a month, buy grey material and sew your own uniform.

b) Follow the battles and take the uniforms off your dead friends.

2 You are Orion Howe, a Unionist soldier. The army refuses to give you a rifle because you are too small. Instead you are made a drummer. Drumbeats tell the soldiers which direction to move on the battlefield. Where do you position yourself?

a) Beside the commander in charge of the troops, half a mile behind the fighting where your drumming can still be heard.

b) In the middle of your troops because your drumming helps to keep them closer together. Of course the enemy will try to shoot you.

3 You are a young Unionist soldier and you have been captured by the Confederates. The food in the prison camp is dreadful but you can buy better food if you can make a

little money. What can you do to earn extra money as a prisoner?

a) Make and sell jewellery.

b) Catch and sell rats.

4 You are a Unionist army surgeon. You are operating on a man with a wound that has turned septic. The knife slips and cuts your own finger. What do you do?

a) Wash the finger and wrap it in a clean bandage.

b) Have another doctor cut your finger off.

5 You are a Unionist soldier, Corporal Thomas Galway, and are at the battle of Gettysburg. The Confederate troops have attacked and been driven back. You chase after them and catch a group of 50 enemy soldiers. What do you do?

a) Grab hold of the nearest one and order him to surrender?

b) Order them all to surrender, even though they outnumber you 50 to one?

Answers: Count the number of **a**)s and **b**)s.

Score 5 **b**)s and you are so tough a tiger would run if he saw you coming.

3–4 **b**)s Good. You are tough enough to fight in the Civil War, but were you honest?

1–2 **b**)s Bad. Stick to embroidery and computer games, but don't go fighting in any real battles.

0 **b**)s Chicken. If you look closely in a mirror you can see a thin yellow streak running down your back. Of course, you could be just too sensible to get yourself killed!

The **b**) answers are all true. Here's what happened…

1 Abel Sheeks wasn't happy about taking the clothing off dead men. He said, 'I always believed the dead should not be disturbed.' But he did it because he had to, and in a few weeks he had a uniform as good as anyone else in the Confederate army. Abel was just 16 years old.

2 Orion Howe was just 14 when he became a drummer. He was hit several times during the Battle of Vicksburg but kept drumming and earned a Medal of Honour. Johnny Clem was only 11 when he ran away from home and joined the Unionist army and by the age of 12 he'd had two drums smashed by shell-fire. He couldn't drum so he picked up a musket and started shooting back. Johnny fought bravely for the rest of the war.

3 Prisoners did use a rubbery tree sap called gutta percha to make simple rings and brooches. They also made tooth-picks from old bones and sold them to buy corn meal, sugar and coffee. But an easier trade was in rats. A young Unionist soldier wrote, 'We are so short of food that many prisoners are in the rat trade, either selling these horrid animals or killing them and eating them. They are so tame they hardly think it worth their while to get out of our way when we meet them.'

4 The doctor was afraid that the infection from the patient's wound would get into his own bloodstream. He immediately had another surgeon operate to remove his finger. Just as well the knife didn't slip and cut his head!

5 Corporal Galway had a badly bruised thigh, but limped after the enemy and called on them to surrender. Even though he was alone, he rounded up all 50 of the enemy and took them back as prisoners of war. Thomas Galway was just 15 years old at the time.

Foul fighting facts

War can be dreadfully disgusting. It wasn't just enemy shells and bullets and bayonets you had to worry about. There were…

1 Clumsy comrades The first shots in the Civil War were fired at Fort Sumter. Over 4,000 shells were fired in 34 hours of fighting … and no one was killed! But the walls were battered and the Unionist troops inside knew they had to surrender. The Confederates allowed the beaten men to lower their flag and fire a cannon salute of 50 guns. In a freak explosion two of the Unionist troops were killed by their own cannon. The first victims of the Civil War had managed to kill themselves!

(The Confederates were just as bad. Confederate soldiers shot their own General Jackson at the Battle of Chancellorsville in 1863. It was getting dark at the time, they thought he was a Unionist soldier and they said it was a simple *mistake*. So that's all right – except for General Jackson, of course!)

2 Dire diseases Some historians have reckoned that more people died of sickness than died of wounds during the war. By the end of the war, most new soldiers were given the measles before joining the fighting men. That was so they wouldn't fall sick when they were needed to fight. (This makes sense – your own army spotted you before the enemy had a chance to spot you.)

3 Creepy-crawlies Between battles the soldiers often became bored in their camps. They passed the time by gambling. Cards were popular but racing was more exciting. Foot races were organized and so were horse races. When the men were really desperate they took a louse from their uniform and had louse races! (Just as exciting as horse races ... but it must have been hard to find jockeys small enough!)

4 Sore soles Between battles the soldiers often had to march a long distance over rough, stony roads. Their problem was their boots fell apart and they had to try to carry on barefoot. If they lagged behind they would be in trouble. One straggler told his general, 'I tried walking barefoot but my feet just kept bleeding. My heart is loyal and true ... but my feet ain't. Of course I could have crawled on my hands and knees, but then my hands would have been too sore to fire my rifle.' He was forgiven. (You may like to try this excuse on your teacher: 'My heart is in my homework ... but my brain ain't.')

5 Rotten racists Two hundred thousand black soldiers fought for the Unionist armies in the Civil War. Were the soldiers and the citizens of the north grateful? Not really. There was a race riot in New York in 1863 and a black boy was killed. The boy's uncle, Sergeant Robert Simmons, died in a battle just three days later, fighting for the people who had murdered his nephew and beaten up his mother and sister. The white soldiers often treated the black soldiers badly, even though the black soldiers fought as bravely as anyone. Black soldiers got less pay and worse food.

6 Foul food In the 1854 siege of St Petersburg the soldiers were forced to survive on biscuits known as 'hardtack'. The trouble was, most of these biscuits were riddled with worms. The sickened soldiers threw them away. An officer visited the trenches where the soldiers had dug their shelters. He was horrified to

see the biscuits lying there. 'This hardtack will attract rats and mice. You can't just drop your biscuits anywhere! Throw the stuff out of the trenches!'

One of the soldiers called back, 'We've thrown those biscuits away two or three times but they just keep crawling back!'

The French Revolution

First the Americans revolted against Britain. Then the French went to help the Americans, because they didn't like the Brits much (nothing changes).

But wars cost money and the French pockets were penniless (or franc-less to be frank). The poor peasants were forced to pay taxes they couldn't afford. Then they had an idea...

OUR AMERICAN FRIENDS HAD UNFAIR TAXES, DIDN'T THEY?

AND THEY REVOLTED AND WON!

SO WHY CAN'T WE FRENCH?

French Revolution timeline

DOWN WITH THE TOFFS

1789 French peasants have had enough of being pushed around by the posh people. They starve while the nobles fill their faces. They rebel in the countryside while a mob attacks the Bastille Prison in Paris.

1791 French King Louis XVI tries to run for his life but he's caught and returned to Paris with his hated Queen, Marie Antoinette. Luckless Louis appears in front of the people's parliament and how do they show they are free men? By keeping their hats *on* as he comes in when they should have removed them to show respect! Shock! Horror!

1792 France declares war on Austria to stop her king coming to Louis' rescue. France declares it's a king-free country – a republic – and defeats the invading army. It's not just France against her King any more – it's France against every country with a king.

1793 King Louis is executed on the new machine – the guillotine. It's the start of 'the Terror' in which 30,000 people will be executed. France is at war with Britain, Holland and Spain … who would like to see Louis' head stuck back on. Marie Antoinette's head follows her husband's into the basket nine months later.

1794 This war costs money and that means more taxes. But that's why the Revolution started in the first place. So now there are revolutions against the Revolution! 'Terror' leader Robespierre goes to the guillotine and the Terror dies down a little.

1799 A young general called Napoleon Bonaparte says, 'The revolution is over!' (It isn't.) 'You will all do what the army tells you!' (They do.)

1804 Now Napoleon says, 'What you really need is an emperor. Me, in fact.' He stages an election and gets himself elected. He even puts on his own crown at the coronation.

But the wars go on as Napoleon and his French armies decide to take over the world (with help from their American friends).

1812 The French attack Russia in winter. Big mistake. Frozen French noses and toeses. The soldiers slowly starve while Napoleon eats white bread, beef and mutton. I'm all right, Jacques!

1815 Brits finally beat Napoleon at Waterloo (the battlefield in Belgium not the station in London). Napoleon is sent into exile while France gets a king again – Louis XVIII – the little brother of chopped Louis XVI.

1830 Now King Charles X tries to get bossy and the French revolt – again.

Pays to be posh

You can understand why the peasants were upset by 1789. They heard the following stories (all true) about the nasty nobles...

• Many peasants struggled to find enough food while the King's friend, Madame Tallien, liked to bathe in crushed strawberries whenever she could.

• Most peasants shared a pathetic cottage with their animals. King Louis XVI's Versailles Palace was 580 metres wide.

• A whole village of peasants would share a single well for water – Versailles had 1,000 fountains supplied by 100 miles of pipes.

• The laws for the people were harsh. Lord de Pelier went to prison for 50 years because he dared to whistle at Queen Marie Antoinette.

• The poorest peasants paid taxes – the richest bishops and lords paid nothing.

It's not surprising that the people of France were fed up.

Anyway, the French decided to nobble the nobles with a machine called a guillotine.

The machine was first used on a highwayman. The highwayman didn't argue with that and neither did the hundreds of nobles who went the same way. The guillotine was last used to execute a murderer in 1939. Then it got the chop.

The bloodbath

A wise old proverb says, 'Those who live by the sword die by the sword.' And those who live by a bloodbath can sometimes die in a bloody bath. That's what happened to a leader of the French Revolution, Jean Paul Marat.

If there'd been a daily newspaper in Paris at the time then the horrible headlines would have been about the execution of charming Charlotte Corday, the cut-throat killer!

PARIS EVENING POST

3p – une Bargain

17 JULY 1793

CHARLOTTE CHOPPED!

MARAT'S MURDERER GETS IT IN THE MUSH!

There was a sensation at the execution of Charlotte Corday in Paris today.

No sooner had her brain box hit the basket than the executioner snatched it out and punched it in the face.

Charlotte was an enemy of Revolutionary leader Jean Paul Marat. Last week she asked to see the great man and found the mucky Marat in the bath where he usually worked. First she named a list of traitors and he wrote them down and promised to have them guillotined. But there was a nasty surprise for John-Paul. The greatest traitor of all was Charlotte herself! She drew a kitchen knife from her skirt and stabbed him to death. The mad murderess was arrested on the spot and sentenced to die on the guillotine. Today the execution was carried out in the presence of a huge crowd at the Paris chopping centre, Place de la Révolution. But the executioner didn't realize how popular the charming Charlotte was. When he put a fist in her face there was almost a riot in the angry crowd. The man has already been fined for misconduct.

Revolutionary rule: Trust nobody

Charlotte Corday got close to Jean-Paul Marat by pretending to be a supporter. But she wasn't the first or the last to try this.

In 1584, a Catholic pretended to be a Protestant and got close to Dutch rebel leader, William of Orange. He shot him. (William of Orange had been nicknamed 'William the Silent' – after meeting the Catholic crack-shot he became William the Very Silent.)

The Terror

The French invented 'the Terror' in their 1789 Revolution. The Revolutionaries decided the best way to get rid of old enemies was to kill them. Many royals and nobles were executed on the guillotine but the Revolutionaries soon turned their murdering hands on anyone who opposed them.

When the Austrian enemy started to invade France, the ordinary people went wild with panic and started a Terror of their own. They killed…

- **Priests** because they were from the old Catholic Church that had supported the King.

- **Nobles in prison** because they had been friends of the royal family. Madam de Lamballe was taken from her prison, had her head hacked off and stuck on a pole. The trophy was then taken to be shown to the King and Queen in their prison.

- **Madwomen and orphan girls** whose only crime was to live in the poorhouse that the Catholic Church had provided for them.

- **Ordinary criminals, thieves, tricksters and highwaymen** These villains must have thought they were safe, tucked away in their miserable, damp, cold little cells. The mob broke in, gave them ridiculous 'trials', condemned them to death and butchered them in all sorts of cruel ways.

• **Revolutionary leaders** They turned against any leaders who said, 'Hang on, let's not kill so many people here!' One person who tried to cool the Terror was Georges Danton. In the end he was brought to trial; when he argued too strongly he was told to shut up. He said…

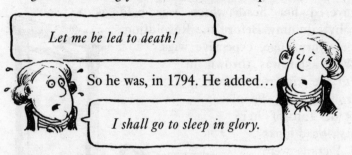

Let me be led to death!

So he was, in 1794. He added…

I shall go to sleep in glory.

He is still waiting to be woken up.

Chop and change

Executioners who used an axe could be rotten shots and a real pain in the neck. So the guillotine was a great invention. Impress your teacher with these grisly guillotine facts…

1 It was named after its inventor, Doctor Joseph-Ignace Guillotin … unlike the electric chair, the lethal injection, the firing squad or the lay-down-in-the-middle-of-the-road-while-I-run-over-you-in-this-steamroller – none of which was named after its inventor.

2 The chopping machine wasn't always called a guillotine. At first it was named a Louisette or a Louison – which is daft. After King Louis XVI was executed the name should have been changed from Louison to Louis-off. Criminals later nicknamed it 'the Widow'.

3 Doctor Joseph-Ignace Guillotin (who did not get the idea from working in a bacon-slicing factory) said that all the victim felt was a chill on the back of the neck. Not one of his victims has ever argued.

4 The machine was tested on corpses from a local hospital, which is a dead good idea.

5 The machine's first live victim was a highwayman who was sliced in 1792. One day he was holding up stage coaches, the next day he couldn't even hold his head up.

6 When the French Queen, Marie Antoinette, was executed, she went to the guillotine in a white cap. This covered her head which was bald as a baby's dummy. Before the Revolution she wore huge, expensive wigs. When she was thrown in jail the wigs were taken from her. People made fun of her slap-head looks.

7 Victims were not expected to walk to the guillotine. They were carried along in a small cart known as a tumbrel (though some people call it tumbril. If you are off to be beheaded you are not going to argue about the spelling). These tumbrels had been used by the peasants to carry animal droppings. At least having your head cut off would get the smell out of your nose.

THIS REVOLUTION IS A REAL PAIN IN THE NECK!

8 There was a rule that said Frenchwomen should be taught about the Revolution. They were encouraged to take their knitting to the executions and watch. One woman who cashed in on the Terror was Madame Marie Tussaud.

She made 'death masks' of the famous heads and took them fresh from the guillotine basket. Marie Tussaud took her collection on tour around Britain for over 30 years before setting up her famous waxworks in London. Many of the severed heads belonged to her friends ... but this didn't stop her making wax copies for her exhibition. This is a bit like you taking your poor dead pet goldfish, frying it and selling it with chips for a profit.

SHE'S CERTAINLY GOT A HEAD FOR HEIGHTS!

9 The Revolution's leaders brought in a law which said workers could be paid only so much and no more – the 'maximum'. This rule was terribly unpopular and the mob who went to the executions detested it. So, as they watched heads roll they didn't shout, 'Off with his head!' or 'Chuck that head over here so we can have a game of netball!' No, the French mob shouted, 'Down with the maximum!'

10 The city of Lyon suffered mass guillotine sessions because few people there had supported the Revolution. The guillotine couldn't get through the necks quickly enough so the Revolutionaries brought in good old firing

squads to help kill more. In Nantes they filled barges with condemned people, towed them into the middle of the river and sank them so their victims drowned.

This horrible history of the guillotine makes the executioners and the audience sound sick and disgusting. In fact, the mob who gathered to gloat could have sensitive little stomachs. In Nantes, the magistrates ordered that the guillotines should be painted red. Then the blood wouldn't show up and the mob wouldn't be sickened by the gory splashes!

I LIKE A GOOD GUILLOTINING, BUT I CAN'T STAND ALL THAT MESS

KNIT KNIT

   This rule doesn't make a lot of sense, does it? If anyone hated the sight of blood then all they had to do was stay away from the executions.

Chop shop

Leader of the French Revolution, Maximilien-François-Marie-Isidore de Robespierre, was accused of becoming a dictator ... just as bad as the King he'd had executed. The Revolutionaries turned against their leader and decided to have Robespierre executed.

   Now Robespierre didn't fancy the idea of going to the guillotine, so he took a pistol and tried to shoot himself in the head. You'd think it would be difficult to miss your own head, wouldn't you? But Robespierre did. The shot just smashed his jaw. Within a week he was taken to the guillotine with a bandaged jaw.

An eyewitness described Robespierre's execution…

At four o'clock in the afternoon the sinister procession came from the courtyard of the Palace of Justice. No crowd of this size had ever been seen in Paris before. Most of the watchers fixed their eyes on the cart where Robespierre was riding. The miserable creature was all mutilated and covered with blood. Robespierre kept his eyes shut and didn't open them again till he was being carried up to the scaffold. The wretched man's head was now no more than an object of horror and disgust. When at last it was separated from his body, and the executioner took it by the hair to show it to the people, it presented an indescribably horrible sight.

In all, 108 people died for supporting Robespierre – but his execution got more cheers than the rest put together. Popular little man.

Cool caps

If you're a revolutionary then it helps to know who your fellow revolutionaries are. After all, it wouldn't do to go shooting someone who turns out to have been one of your supporters.

Your enemies, the government forces, will have uniforms. Your revolutionaries need some sort of symbol too. The French Revolution came up with one of the best ones – the Phrygian cap.

This is a soft felt or wool cone that fits closely around the head and has its pointed crown curling forward.

It originated in the ancient country of Phrygia in Asia. In Rome, the Phrygian cap was worn by freed slaves as a symbol of their freedom.

During the French Revolution, it was adopted by the Revolutionaries as 'the red cap of liberty'. And in the French Communard Revolution 80 years later it was used again.

Make your own Red Cap of Liberty

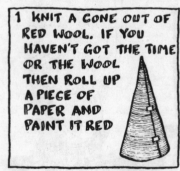

> *Horrible Histories* health warning: Wearing the Red Cap of Liberty will make sure your revolutionary friends know you are one of them. Unfortunately the red cap also makes you a perfect target for government snipers. A bullet through the cap will ruin it ... and it won't do much for your head either.

Did you know...?

France, 1789 At the start of the French Revolution a mob attacked the Bastille prison. It was guarded by a drawbridge and the rebels let this fall with a crash.

Unfortunately, one of the mob was standing underneath it when it fell. He was flattened like a hedgehog under a juggernaut's wheel. It must have spoiled his revolutionary sense of adventure.

Eire today and gone tomorrow

Once you've got a good revolution going then you want to share it around a bit. The French started spreading their troublemaking ideas and this upset the British who went to war with them – the Napoleonic Wars.

In 1798, the United Irishmen plotted a revolution against their British rulers. They asked the French for help and the French sent 20 ships – they were always glad of an excuse to attack the English. Strong winds drove the ships back to France and left the United Irishmen at the mercy of the avenging British forces.

The Brits demanded to know which people in the town were members of the rebel United Irishmen group. If a prisoner refused to talk then he was tortured.

Which torture would you prefer? Which could you stand for the longest? Take your picket first...

Picketing

The victim is hanged by one arm over a wooden picket – a pole carved to a sharp point. The only way to rest the arm is to take your weight by putting a foot on the sharp spike.

Would you suffer or call, 'Let me down!' and betray your friends?

Flogging

The victim is tied to a wooden frame and flogged with a leather whip with nine lashes on it – a cat-o'-nine-tails. Two hundred or more lashes were common. The only way to stop the lashing was to tell the torturer the names of your rebel friends. Some United Irishmen betrayed a whole town rather than suffer the lashing.

It's not surprising. A ten-year-old boy witnessed a man being flogged till his flesh was torn to shreds and he begged to be shot. Men were flogged till their ribs, spine and liver could be seen.

Would you suffer or cry 'Stop!' and betray your friends?

Pitch-capping

A brown paper cap was filled with melted tar and jammed on the head of the victim. It was then left to cool and set firmly in the hair. When it had hardened it was set alight and the victim released for sport. The melting, scalding pitch would run down his face and into his eyes; the only way to take the cap off was to tear away the hair and scalp.

Would you suffer or call, 'Pour water on my head!' and betray your friends?

Rotten rebels

Robert Emmet was an Irish rebel leader. Unfortunately for the Irish, Robert Emmet and his men were as bright as a candle under water.

The British forces sat in Dublin Castle, knowing an attack was planned but not knowing when it would come. They waited for their spies to bring them news.

First the landlord of a pub arrived to tell the Brits that he'd heard men talking about the rebellion and it was due to start that night. That was careless ... but the other mistakes were simply daft.

A factory owner who was a friend of the British arrived at the castle with news...

And that wasn't the only clumsy mistake that doomed the rebels...

• They had a supply of explosives – but they accidentally set them off a week before the date of the rising.

• As the rising started they armed themselves with grenades – but no one could find the fuses to set them off.

• Many failed to join the rebellion because a message arrived to say, 'It's off!' – but the messenger was a traitor sent by the British, and the Irish believed him and went home.

• They planned to climb the walls of Dublin Castle – but at the last minute discovered there was only one ladder.

• A rebel fired a pistol and scared the horses that were supposed to take them to Dublin Castle – they bolted and left the rebels to walk.

• The rebels were told that soldiers were approaching – they rushed out to find it was just a crowd of Irish drunks coming out of the pubs at closing time.

• Leader Robert Emmet called off the rebellion before it had really started and went into hiding. He was caught, hanged and cut into quarters. His supporters tried to dip handkerchiefs in the martyr's blood as a souvenir ... but dogs beat them to it and lapped it all up!

When Robert Emmet was taken to the scaffold for treason he climbed the ladder and had the rope placed round his neck. It was the executioner's job to take the ladder away. The executioner asked, 'Are you ready, sir?' and Emmet said, 'Not yet!' This was repeated several times. Emmet said, 'Not yet!' for the last time but the hangman was so fed up with waiting he took the ladder away anyway. Emmet died saying, 'Not ye ... cccct!'

And talking about famous last words...

Dead pathetic

If you are going to die in a revolution then at least try to make sure you are *remembered*. The best way to do this is to have some famous last words. But some rebellious last words are, quite honestly, not up to scratch...

1431 Joan of Arc cried 'Jesus!' as she burned. Jesus mustn't have had a fire-extinguisher handy and didn't save her. (Maybe Joan should have called on Jesus's mother, Mary. As Bohemian rebels threw the emperor's men out of the palace windows one cried, 'Jesu! Maria! Help!' He landed safely in a rubbish heap beneath the window and the rebels gasped, 'By God! His Mary has helped!')

1541 Francisco Pizarro also cried 'Jesus'. He was hacked down but had time to draw a cross on the earth in his own blood. He then kissed the cross, said his famous last word and died.

1555 As Bishop Hugh Latimer was burned by Mary Tudor for being a Protestant rebel he turned to his fellow victim and said, 'We shall this day light such a candle in England as shall never be put out.' The other 'candle' probably thought, 'Hugh get on my wick.'

1610 Henry IV of France was assassinated by a mad monk François Ravaillac. The King was caught in a traffic jam so the murdering monk jumped on his carriage and stabbed him twice in the chest. What did the dying King say? 'I've been stabbed!' Brilliant!

1794 French Revolutionary George Danton was just as daft. As he was led off to execution he cried, 'Take us to the guillotine now!' Well, they weren't going to take him off to a picnic in Paris, were they? Anyway, not everyone in his group of victims agreed! Danton's colleague, Desmoulins's famous last words were not so brave. They were something like, 'Save us! Help! I don't want to die! Boo! Hoo!'

1799 Rebel American leader George Washington said, 'I am not afraid to go.' This is just as well because he didn't have much choice. He went.

Did you know...?
Joan of Arc wasn't the only battling Frenchwoman. In the 1789 French Revolution many women took weapons and went to fight in the battle of Valmy. Often these heroines were dressed only in rags but they faced the enemy as bravely as the men alongside them.

The French rewarded them by banning them from future battles. The women who were still in the army were told to go home. They were paid the tiny amount of one sou for every five kilometres they had to walk back.

The Revolution was controlled by groups called 'clubs'. The women had their own Republican Women's Clubs until they were banned in 1793. Some of the Women's Club leaders went to the guillotine.

And the French Revolution was supposed to make everyone 'equal'. As always this meant every *man* would be made equal.

Nasty 19th century

The 19th century was a time for copycats. The French had a fun revolution in the 1790s and in the next hundred years it seems that everyone wanted to have their own. In fact, the French got such a taste for revolution they kept bringing their kings and emperors back just so they could have the pleasure of revolting all over again.

The Europeans made British attempts at rebellion look pretty tame. 1848, for example, was the 'year of revolutions' with serious trouble in Italy, Austria, Hungary and Germany. Of course the French, who believed they invented revolutions, couldn't be left out. They threw out their king ... again ... and elected a Napoleon ... again. But in England the great revolt was a wash-out – literally. The Chartist march in London was a failure because heavy rain kept the protestors at home. What a wet lot!

And the Chinese were worse. In 1850 their Taiping Revolution began. In the next 15 years it would lead to the destruction of 600 cities and the deaths of 20 million people – twice as many as the First World War was to kill between 1914 and 1918.

Other horrible highlights of the sad century included...

Nasty 19th-century timeline

1871 Power to the people of Paris. The Communards of Paris declare they are running the city and the country after the shocking defeat in the war against Germany. In the battles that follow, the French government kill far more Frenchmen than the German soldiers ever did – 20,000 to 30,000 are killed or executed.

1875 The Turkish or Ottoman Empire has been going since the 13th century. Now it's starting to fall apart. The Bulgarian peasants revolt and 12,000 are butchered.

1876 The Sioux Indians in Dakota are rebelling against the American settlers. General George Custer rides to the Little Big Horn River with his 256 troopers, expecting to massacre a few Indians. Instead he finds a huge Sioux army. Oooops! The troopers shoot their own horses for cover so have nothing to escape on. They're massacred by Sioux led by Crazy Horse – one horse they failed to shoot.

1881 Russian Tsar Alexander II is blown up and US President James Garfield is shot. Garfield survived the assassin's bullet ... then died of blood poisoning because the doctors used dirty instruments when they took the bullet out.

Vile for Victorians

So what drove the Brits to the brink of revolution in the reign of Queen Victoria?

When you look at the dreadful conditions poor people suffered in Victorian Britain it's surprising the Chartist rebels didn't succeed. Take food, for example...

Tasteless tapioca

Mrs Martha Gordon published a book called *Cooking for Working Men's Wives* and gave this recipe...

111

Tapioca pie

Ingredients

10 0g. beef dripping
225g onions, sliced
1.6 kg potatoes, sliced
7.5g tapioca
Salt and pepper
225g plain flour
1 teaspoon baking powder

Method

Soak the tapioca for an hour in cold water.
Take a quarter of the dripping and put it on the bottom of a pie dish.
Add a layer of onion, potato, tapioca, salt and pepper.
Mix the flour, baking powder and the remains of the dripping.
Add water till it makes a smooth dough.
Roll it out and make a smooth lid for the pie.
Bake it at level 6 (20°c) for about 70 -80 minutes.

You might like to try cooking this just to have a taste of being poor in Victorian times.

Remember, you can have only *one* piece of this pie, which has been cut into six pieces. Wash it down with water and eat nothing else for the rest of the day.

Hungry and irritated? Feel like rebelling? The Victorian Brits didn't get angry enough. Of course schools taught them to be grateful for what they had. Children were taught the value of food at school with this little rhyme...

I must not throw upon the floor
The crust I cannot eat;
For many little hungry ones
Would think it quite a treat.

My parents labour very hard
To get me wholesome food;
Then I must never waste a bit
That would do others good.

For awful waste makes awful want
And I may live to say,
'Oh! How I wish I had the bread
That I once threw away.'

Note: The song is chanted with hand signs – throwing an imaginary piece of bread, rubbing an empty stomach and so on.

Fat fools

Most revolutions could be avoided. If the leaders would only try to understand the problems of the peasants. It's dreadful when your leader doesn't listen…

SORRY I HAVEN'T GOT MY HOMEWORK, BUT THE DOG ATE IT…

AND THERE'S A FLOCK OF PIGS FLYING PAST THE WINDOW

Queen Victoria's British army were really bad listeners.

113

Fourteen thousand British troops ruled 150 *million* people in India. The Brits had the help of almost 300,000 Indian soldiers in running the country. But the Brits were so stupid they upset the people they should have been working with – they upset the Indian soldiers.

Those Indians became more and more angry as the Brits became more and more deaf!

In 1853 the British Army controlled India. But a new invention was about to bring trouble...

And so the Indian Mutiny started – 14 months of bitter fighting and dreadful slaughter.

But it wasn't caused by the fat *bullets* – it was caused by the fat *heads* who commanded the army.

Did you know…?
In 1885 there was a rebellion in the Sudan against the British army. The Dervish natives were fighting with spears against British guns but some Dervish warriors still got through. A gunner had to pack gunpowder into the barrel of his gun with a wooden 'rammer'. This took time. While one gunner was ramming powder down, a Dervish attacked him with a spear. The gunner snatched his rammer out of the barrel and smashed it down on the head of the attacker.

Next day an officer called the gunner in front of him and demanded, 'Why did you smash that rammer? Rammers cost money!'

'Sorry, sir,' the gunner groaned. 'I didn't mean to do it. I just never realized the Dervishes had such hard heads!'

Or that Queen Victoria's army was so mean!

Hanging around for Hong

Hong Xiuquan called himself the Heavenly King and led a revolution against the mighty Manchu family who ruled China – the Taiping Revolution. For 15 years Hong Xiuquan ruled a kingdom of his own.

He was deadlier than a rottweiler with a razor.

In 1864 Hong Xiuquan was beaten by his enemies who besieged him in the city of Nanjing. Did he lead his troops into battle? No. He sat in his palace and invented new ways of executing his own people … and the biggest crime was forgetting to call Hong Xiuquan 'heavenly'.

When his people began to starve he told them to 'eat sweet dew'.

At last the message got through to hopeless Hong: 'You are beaten. You are yesterday's news.'

So Hong Xiuquan decided to take poison. Ordinary poison wasn't good enough for a heavenly king so he swallowed gold leaf. (Do not try this at home by swallowing your dad's gold watch. It won't kill you but he'll give you a right ticking off while you try to pass the time.)

Before the enemies broke into the city to massacre the Taiping rebels they buried Hong Xiuquan in the garden of his palace. Most people would be happy having flowers around their grave, but the Heavenly King had trees ... and from every tree there dangled Hong Xiuquan's many wives. They'd hanged themselves because they couldn't bear to live without him ... a bit like Romeo and several Juliets.

Isn't that sweet?

119

Smoke gets in your eyes

By 1881 Tsar Alexander II of Russia had been the target of more assassination attemps than probably any other leader. And he was one of the *better* Russian emperors. When Tsar Alex took the throne, Russia still had 30 million 'serfs' – peasants who could be bought or sold and were little more than slaves. He gave them their freedom, and still the revolutionaries weren't content. They wanted him dead as a duck's toenail.

They shot at him in his royal palace, in his royal train and in his royal carriage, and missed – though they killed a horse that got in the way. They tried to bomb him in his dining room – but only succeeded in killing soldiers and servants.

Finally the revolutionaries, who called themselves Anarchists, came up with a double-bomb plot that reached the parts other bombers failed to reach.

Tsar Alexander had just signed the document that would let his people vote for the Council of the Empire when the commander of his guards warned him, 'Don't go to the army parade tomorrow. It's too dangerous.'

Alex ignored the advice and set off in his carriage. He inspected his troops and drove off to lunch with his cousin. No one tried to harm him.

When he finally set off for his palace he drove past groups of spectators in the streets. A woman waved a handkerchief – the Tsar waved back, but she wasn't waving at him. She was waving a signal to her Anarchist friends.

A man ran from the crowd and threw a bundle, wrapped in a newspaper, under the horses' feet where it exploded in a cloud of smoke and snow. When the snow settled it was stained with the blood of two horses, two guards and an innocent butcher's boy who'd been watching the procession.

But the Tsar wasn't hurt. His carriage windows were shattered but he was unharmed. He wanted to speak to the injured. Someone in the crowd called out...

That's when the second bomber stepped from the crowd and said...

...before flinging a second bomb at the Tsar. It tore gaping wounds in his legs and chest. The monarch struggled to his feet and managed to say…

TAKE ME HOME TO THE PALACE TO DIE!

That's what his guards did – and that's what Alexander II did a few hours later.

Alex's son took over and the dead Tsar's plan to give Russians the vote was scrapped. The revolutionaries got themselves a worse life, not a better one. Of course, Alex had no life at all.

Horrible historical joke:

IF THE KING OF RUSSIA IS CALLED A TSAR AND THE QUEEN IS A TSARINA, WHAT DO YOU CALL THE LITTLE PRINCES AND PRINCESSES?

TSARDINES!

Crazy communards

The Communards were the workers of Paris and in 1871 they rebelled against the Emperor's government. They had no real organization and not much idea about how to fight a revolutionary war against the Emperor's army. What they lacked in skill they made up for in cruelty.

Cock-eyed Communards

In 1871 the people of Paris formed their own army to fight their Emperor's army. Wisely they pinched 200 of the Emperor's cannon and took them up to the top of a hill where they could bombard the enemy.

The Emperor sent a troop of soldiers to recapture them.

Before dawn on 18 March, the guns were taken without a fight, as all the sentries were asleep! Stupid and careless Communards.

Then the Emperor's men discovered that nobody had brought any teams of horses to drag away the guns. Careless and stupid soldiers.

So they waited and were soon surrounded by an angry crowd. Some young soldiers mutinied and joined the mob, others defended themselves with their bayonets, but their leader, General Lecomte, was dragged from his horse and taken for interrogation to a house.

Then another captured General – Clement Thomas – was brought to the house. The mob demanded their deaths. They were tried on a show of hands and dragged into the back garden. There was no proper firing squad and the first ragged volley of shots failed to kill Thomas. Shot after shot was fired at him until a bullet hit him in the eye. Lecomte was killed with one bullet in the back.

The mob then mutilated the bodies.

Ten things you'd rather not know about the Communards

1 Communard Police Chief Rigault was only 26 years old but looked about 40. He was short and stocky with a round face, a bushy black beard and a cruel smile. When enemy soldiers shot him, his naked body was left in a gutter for two days to be kicked and spat on. His girlfriend finally covered it with a coat.

SNIFFLE

SOB

IT WAS MY FAVOURITE COAT... SNIFF

2 The Communards had treated their victims no better. When they executed the Bishop of Paris they threw his

body into a ditch by the Père-Lachaise cemetery to rot. In revenge the Emperor's army took 147 Communards to the cemetery and shot them. (At least it saved carrying their bodies to their graves.)

3 The Communard firing squads were clumsy. They took four policemen into a courtyard to be shot ... but hit just one of them. Another escaped in the darkness. A witness said they hunted him 'like a rat'.

4 A British doctor went to help in a Communard hospital. He was horrified to see the doctors use an instrument to pull bullets out of a wound then stir their coffee with the same instrument. Which is most horrible – the blood in the coffee or the coffee in the wounds?

5 A Communard General was killed with a sword blow that split his skull open. His corpse was loaded into a cart full of horse muck and the body carried back to the Emperor's camp. There, a witness said...

125

6 One of the Communard leaders was Charles Delescluze who had been a revolutionary in the 1830 and 1848 revolutions. By the 1871 Communard Revolution he was 62 years old, exhausted by years of imprisonment and dying of a lung disease. When he realized the Communard Revolt was failing he dressed in his best top hat, polished boots and tail coat. Around his waist he wore a bright red sash. He went to a barricade where the fighting was fiercest, climbed to the top, stood there for a moment ... and was shot down. It was the way he'd chosen to go.

7 After Delescluze's death the mob retreated to the slums and the Emperor's troops marched in to take their revenge. A group of 25 women tried to defend their homes by pouring boiling water down on the heads of the enemy soldiers. They were captured and shot. The Emperor's soldiers also sought out people with dirty, sooty hands because they believed they had been setting fire to the buildings; they found one man with really black hands and shot him dead on the spot. But the poor man was an innocent chimney sweep.

8 A thousand Communards were rounded up and marched out of Paris to the Emperor's camp. Not all of them made it. An English witness said...

> *Old men, women, girls and boys — some nearly in rags — were driven on by the horse-soldiers. I saw two soldiers guarding two young men who were being hissed by the crowd. Suddenly the soldiers clubbed them down with the butt end of their rifles, placed a pistol in an ear of each one and pulled the trigger.*

9 The Emperor's commander, General Gallifet, said to his Communard prisoners…

> *You people may think that I am cruel. But I am even crueller than you can imagine.*

He proved it with some incredible orders.

I**N THE NAME OF HIS IMPERIAL HIGHNESS THE FOLLOWING ORDERS MUST BE OBEYED.**

- **SOLDIERS MUST SHOOT ALL MEN WITH GREY HAIR — SINCE THESE MEN ALMOST CERTAINLY REBELLED IN 1848.**

- **SOLDIERS MUST SHOOT ANYONE WEARING A WATCH — SINCE THESE PEOPLE ARE PROBABLY OFFICERS OF THE COMMUNARDS.**

General Gallifet.

You can imagine this gave rise to a totally new revolutionary cry…

But the most worrying order of all (for someone like you, anyway) was Gallifet's decision that Imperial Soldiers should shoot anyone who was unusually ugly!

10 When the Communards realized it was all over they took their prisoners out of their cells and shot them. Later, a body was found with 69 bullets in it. Another had been stabbed with a bayonet 70 times. *That's* what you call hatred.

Now all this may seem like the most gruesome scene you could imagine. You wouldn't want to go and see the carts full of the dead being trundled out of the city or smell the flesh burning on the huge funeral fires, would you?

You wouldn't … but many English people did. No sooner had the fighting ended than Thomas Cook organized tours to see the death and destruction of Paris.

Piddling in Paris

Revolutions have been fought to change the world people lived in. When the rebels took over the government they changed many old laws. But the Communard rebels of 1871 passed a curious new law...

Piddling Parisians didn't produce as much pee as the dogs and horses in the city. Sometimes revolutions come up with daft new rules.

Spotted spy

Not everyone forgives spies easily. If they are caught, then the people they spied on can give them some very rough justice.

During the 1871 Paris Commune revolt there were government spies in the midst of the rebels. They must have been very nervous, especially after what happened to one of their colleagues called Vincenzoni...

From: A Secret Address
Somewhere outside Paris
26th February 1871

To: The Captain
The Emperor's Police
Secret Headquarters just
outside Paris

My Captain,
   I am writing this report on our friend
Vincenzoni, one of our secret agents in Paris.
Yes, I know we are not supposed to give the names
of agents when we write our reports but it doesn't
matter much for poor Vincenzoni. Not now.
   As instructed we attended the huge march-past of
the National Guard which was followed by a
Republican rally. Suddenly Vincenzoni was spotted
and dragged from the crowd. They forgot all about
the rally and turned on our friend. Of course he
realized what was happening and tried to get
free. He never had a chance. The mob dragged
him to the banks of the Seine, they tied him
hand and foot, and took turns in beating him.
Then he did something no secret policeman
should do. He looked at me and spoke to me!
   "Shoot me!" he cried.
   Some of the women looked at me. "He was
talking to you!" they said.
   "Couldn't have been!" I laughed. "I've never seen
him in my life!"
   I was saved because the mob began to chant, "In
the Seine! In the Seine! In the Seine!" and everyone
turned back to see what was happening. Poor
Vincenzoni was being carried, like a parcel, across
a line of moored barges, and then they dropped
him in the water.
   He sort of bobbed like a cork but he didn't
drown. The current washed him back to the river
bank. Of course, as soon as he landed the crowd

started to stone him and drove him back into the water. And that's where he finally drowned.

This murder lasted over two hours, and it was watched by a crowd of thousands. No one lifted a finger to help him. Not one! Of course, I couldn't. I mean I'm not afraid to die for the emperor but I'm a secret policeman and I couldn't betray myself, could I?

Anyway, Captain, I'm writing to say I'd like to resign. It's not that I'm afraid or anything. And I haven't been scared off by what happened to poor Vincenzoni. It's just that I've been offered a job as a rat-catcher and I've always loved catching rats.

Yours faithfully

Monsieur Bonde (James)

PS: Please send my pay to my Mum.

Vincenzoni's horrible, slow death was seen as a triumph for the Commune. But they didn't have much else to celebrate. Vincenzoni's murder was avenged when over 20,000 Communards were killed in the fighting or executed by firing squads.

Painful for priests

As in the Indian Mutiny of the 19th century, religion was also important in the Communard Revolution. Rebel leaders detested the Catholic Church and Police Chief Rigault took great pleasure in arresting the Archbishop of Paris, Darboy. (This was the beginning of the elimination of priests, including Empress Eugenie's confessor, aged 77, who was caught attempting to escape over his garden wall.)

A Catholic priest was questioned by Rigault and this extract was taken from the report...

But Rigault's days of power didn't last. As we know he came to a nasty end like many other Paris Communard rebels.

Torturing 20th century

Test your teacher with this torturing question…

If they don't get the answer then give them another clue or two…

And if they still don't get it give them one last clue…

When they've failed you can walk away, shaking your head, muttering, 'You've been around for most of the 20th century so I thought you'd know the answer!' (That always annoys them.) Then say that you'll give the answer next week. (That annoys them even more!)

When you at last tell them the answer they will moan (teachers are good at that) and say, 'I knew that!'

Just shake your head wisely and sadly. You know the answer, don't you? Of course, the answer is…

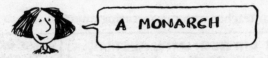

A MONARCH

The 20th century has been a time when kings, queens, tsars, kaisers, emperors and other assorted types of monarch disappeared.

Revolutions before the 20th century often replaced the old monarch with a new one. But the French revolutions showed that people could manage quite well by themselves, thank you very much. They set up power by the people – a republic – and they were led by a President that the people (usually) chose.

In the great wars of the 20th century the losers looked for someone to blame – and the monarch was useful for that.

Some monarchs did better than others. Really torture your teacher with these kruel kingly kwestions. They get a point for every question they get right. They get a bonus point if they can answer: 'Does the country in question have a monarch today?'

Murderous for monarchs

1 Frederick VIII of Denmark died in 1912. In what shocking way did the family find out about his death?
a) When his body crashed through the palace roof and landed on the dining table. (He'd tried to parachute on to the palace roof but it failed to open.)

134

b) They got a call from the German police saying: 'We've got a corpse in the mortuary and we're not sure who it is. We think it may be your King!'

c) They were fishing on the Elbe when his corpse drifted past. He'd been for a swim but was attacked by a shark.

2 King George of Greece was Frederick's brother. After Fred's death in the street what did he do?
a) Refused to ever set foot in a street again.
b) Passed a law banning everyone from the streets of Greece on Wednesdays (when he went for a walk).
c) Went out on the streets and got himself assassinated.

3 In 1903 The Black Hand Gang entered the palace of the Serbian King, Aleksander, to kill him. He hid. What did the Black Hand killers do to the palace staff that they found?
a) Tortured them till they told where the King and Queen were hiding.
b) Painted their hands black and forced them to join the gang.
c) Chopped them up and threw the bits out of the upstairs windows into the palace gardens.

4 King Nikola of Montenegro was thrown off his throne by his powerful nephew, the King of the Serbs. Old Nikola had an odd way of dealing with criminals. What?

a) King Nikola was the judge and he sat under the old tree of justice to try criminals himself.

b) King Nikola was Montenegro's executioner and was an expert hangman.

c) King Nikola gave murderers ten minutes' start then hunted them to death with a pack of hounds.

5 King (or Kaiser) Wilhelm of Germany was a strict ruler. He had his own sister arrested. What was her crime?

a) She beat him at chess.

b) She kicked his cat.

c) She rode a bicycle in public.

6 Kaiser Wilhelm was a cruel man and had a cruel nickname for King Vittorio Emanuele III of Italy. What?

a) Snotty

b) Dwarf

c) Smelly

7 King Alfonso XIII (lucky for some) of Spain was riding in a parade on 13 April 1913 ... with all those 13s he should have known better! An assassin fired at him and missed ... but had a second gun. What did Alfonso do?

a) Charged at the man and disarmed him.

b) Drew a gun of his own and shot him.

c) Jumped to the ground and hid behind the horse which was shot down.

8 Tsar Nicholas II had a close adviser, Gregory Rasputin. In 1916 Rasputin made three predictions about his own murder. Which one came true?

a) 'If I am killed by a peasant then the tsars will rule for hundreds of years.'

b) 'If I'm killed by a Russian noble then the tsars will not be seen in Russia for 25 years.'

c) 'If I'm killed by a member of the royal family the tsar and his family will not last two years.'

9 Kaiser Karl of Hungary lost his throne in 1918 after he was defeated in the First World War. He tried to get back into Hungary in 1920 using what trick?

a) He rode in a train disguised as a workman from Portugal.

b) He pretended he was dead and was carried back to Hungary in a coffin.

c) He drove into Hungary in an ice-cream van carrying bombs disguised as cornets.

10 King Zog of Albania fled from his palace when the Italians invaded in 1939. He ended up in Paris but, when the Second World War started he was a target for Adolf Hitler's German troops. He fled to England for safety. But how did he get out of Paris when the German air force were searching for him?

a) He travelled on a coal train hidden under sacks of coke.

b) He travelled in a red Mercedes car that was identical to one owned by Hitler.

c) He rode a bicycle and towed the Queen in a barrow behind.

Answers: **1b)** King Fred had been walking alone through the streets of Hamburg when he dropped dead. No one knew who the strange man was and it was 24 hours before his worried family heard that he could be the unidentified corpse. Perhaps he should have worn his crown! Denmark *does* have a monarch today.

2c) King George of Greece was assassinated as he walked through the streets of Salonika just a year after Fred his brother died on a walk. You'd think he'd have learned not to walk in the streets, wouldn't you? He was killed by a drunken beggar. Police believed the killer wasn't a revolutionary, but the assassin killed himself before they made sure. And Greece *does not* have a monarch today.

3c) The King and Queen hid safely in a secret cupboard

in their bedroom. The Black Hand Gang murdered the servants. When the Queen thought it was safe she came out and shouted for help. This told the gang where she and the King were. They came back and finished them off. Serbia *does not* have a monarch today – chopped, minced or otherwise.

4a) In 1931 Montenegro was so old-fashioned it was practically in the Middle Ages. The army had just started taking prisoners alive – earlier in the 20th century they preferred killing them and shoving their heads on poles in their capital Cettinje. King Nikola himself wore the ancient costume of a round cap, a jacket with embroidered edges and baggy sleeves, knee-length trousers, white socks and ankle boots. There were no lawyers or courts – just Nik's Tree of Justice. Montenegro *does not* have a monarch today.

5c) The Kaiser's army was defeated in the First World War, Wilhelm got the blame and was thrown out in 1918. It's hard to feel sorry for him. Germany *does not* have a monarch today.

6b) Kaiser Wilhelm not only called the King of Italy 'Dwarf' but went to great trouble to make Vittorio-Emanuele feel bad about his height. The Italian King was just five feet tall, so Kaiser Wilhelm took him to inspect the tallest guards' regiment in his army.

Vittorio-Emanuele handed power over to the Italian army who joined Germany in losing the Second World War.

The King tried to have his son crowned king of Italy in 1946 but the defeated Italians weren't having it. Italy *does not* have a king today.

7a) Alfonso bravely rode the gunman down. The second bullet singed the King's glove and grazed the horse. Alfie pushed ahead and knocked the man to the ground where the police arrested him. But this wasn't a new experience for Alf the 13th. On his wedding day a bomb had been thrown at him and his bride – the blood of the unlucky horses sprayed her dress. He made the same mistake as Charles I of England and argued with his parliament. They forced him to give up the throne in 1931 and Spain lost its monarchy when General Franco won the Civil War. When Franco died in 1975, Spain invited the royal family to return – but didn't give their new king much real power. So Spain *does* have a monarch today.

8c) In December 1916 Rasputin was invited to a party where Prince Felix Yussoupov and his friends planned his murder. First they gave him poisoned cakes – but he lived. So they gave him poisoned wine – and he lived. Then they shot him in the chest – and he got up and chased them. In desperation they shot him down again, kicked his head, smashed his skull with a club and threw him into the freezing River Neva. He finally took the hint and died. But when revolutionaries overthrew his master, the Tsar, a few months later, they dug up Rasputin's body, soaked it in petrol and set fire to it. After the icy river the corpse might have enjoyed a bit of a warm. The Russian royal family were massacred in July 1918. Russia *does not* have a monarch now.

9a) Kaiser Karl got all the way to Budapest without being recognized. Instead of raising an army to throw out the new government he went along to see the new dictator. He took along just *one* man and tried to persuade the dictator to hand back the kingdom. The dictator refused and threw Kaiser Karl out.

He returned two years later but did no better. He died of a heart attack shortly after. Hungary now *does not* have a monarch.

10b) King Zog had been given the Mercedes by Hitler. German aircraft wouldn't dare shoot it in case it was the one belonging to Adolf. His Queen made him sell the car when he got to England, because she hated Hitler. But it was bought by a crook and he lost his money. During the war Albania was taken over by the Communist supporters of Russia. After the war Zog was not invited back. Today Albania *does not* have a monarch.

Of those ten countries eight lost their monarch during the 20th century. Losing a big war is a pretty sure way for a monarch to get the sack and for rebels to take over.

Torturing 20th-century timeline

1900 In China there is the Boxer Rebellion – a knockout idea.

1903 In Russia the Bolshevik group is formed by Vladimir Lenin. This could be the start of something big in 20th-century revolutions.

1905 The Herero people of Namibia killed 123 European settlers last year. Now the German troops drive them into the desert to die of thirst. The brutal order goes out: 'Every Herero, with or without a rifle, with or without cattle, shall be shot.' Exterminating a whole race of people is known as 'genocide' and will become a common 20th-century terror.

1911 Mexican rebels Pancho Villa and Emiliano Zapata easily defeat the government's incompetent troops and President Diaz runs away to Paris. Meanwhile the Chinese Emperor is facing rebellion throughout his lands. That's a bit tough because he's only five years old. The Chinese let him live, but he's their last emperor.

1914 Serbian rebel kills Austrian Archduke. One of thousands of revolutionary assassinations in history. But this one leads to the

First World War, a war that changes the world and leaves millions dead.

1917 The Germans send revolutionary Vladimir Lenin to their enemy, Russia, in the hope that he'll start a revolution that will knock Russia out of the war. It works a treat and Lenin's Bolsheviks take over Russia. The royal family will be assassinated later.

1918 Germany loses the war and the German people are very bitter. They suffered four years of misery for nothing. They blame the government and the King is thrown out.

1923 A German Communist revolution, like the one in Russia, was defeated in 1919. Now a new rebel group is formed. A little man with a silly moustache fires a shot into the air and declares, 'The national revolution has begun!' He is Adolf Hitler and his Nazis will take over Germany … then try to take over the world.

1936 In Spain the army supports a revolution of Nationalists against the government, the Republicans. Rebel leader, General Franco, will win and rule Spain for the next 40 years. Half a million die in the fighting, many more die of the starvation or disease the war brings. Mr Hitler's Nazis help Franco – it's good practice for the war that is coming in 1939.

1940 The Chinese Communists under Mao Zedong rebel against their Japanese invaders with their Hundred Regiments campaign. The Japanese fight back with their 'three all' tactics. No, it's not a football score. It means three 'all' phrases: 'Kill all, burn all, destroy all.' Vicious. By 1949 Mao has set up his revolutionary government for China, which still exists.

1957 The Hungarians try to revolt against the Russian control of their country. The Russians send in tanks to crush the revolt.

1959 In Cuba the Communists, under Fidel Castro, take over. Two years later the US supports an invasion of Castro's Cuba but that comes to a messy and embarrassing end at the landing beach, the Bay of Pigs.

1967 Travelling troublemaker, Ché Guevara, tries to stir up revolution in Bolivia but ends up being shot dead. Meanwhile, in China, rebels against Mao Zedong's revolution are fighting against his Red Guards. Some prisoners have fingers and noses chopped off.

1975 In Cambodia, Pol Pot launches a violent revolution to establish a new communist society. He wants everyone with links to the old government exterminated. So, if you wore glasses then you were given them by the old government

and you had to be shot. The skulls of Pol Pot's victims are piled into pyramids.

1980 In Poland the workers form a group called Solidarity and begin to resist their Communist government. It's the beginning of the end for communism in eastern Europe.

1989 Solidarity defeats the Communists in Poland and the rest of the Communist countries give up communism. It's the end of the century's greatest revolutionary force. But in China the students revolt and the Communists send tanks against them and kill 2,000 in Tiananmen Square, Beijing. Execution for the leaders is a bullet in the back of the head. So much for that.

1990 A mob marches on London and riots against the Poll Tax ... 609 years after the last time they did it. If the government had read their Horrible Histories then they'd have known the English hate the Poll Tax.

1998 Pol Pot dies. But many people believe the struggle for peace in Cambodia isn't over yet.

Right now Revolutions still going on ... and probably will be in 2999. It seems people just like revolting.

Cruel communists

The idea of 'communism' is a pretty attractive one. 'Everyone is equal. Everything is shared.' The only thing that stops it working is that communists are human beings. And human beings always like to think they're a little better than anyone else ... and too many humans don't like sharing what they've got.

So a communist state has to *force* people to be equal and to share and then it's not really communist at all – the bullies who do the forcing have power over the weak ones who are forced. You see the problem?

But that didn't stop millions of people in the 20th century trying to live the communist way – and dying a cruelly communist way too.

Leon Trotsky

Leon was one of the leaders of the 1917 Russian Revolution. That had been brewing for a while...

- In 1905 the Russian Tsar Nicholas promises to give power to the people in a parliament – then breaks his promise. Sailors who believe in communism rebel and throw their officers overboard. (This is cruel because it's very hard climbing back on board a battleship.) Some of the Tsar's officials are murdered but he survives.
- In 1906 a parliament is formed but has very little power. (The Tsar thinks he's being clever, but if brains were gunpowder he wouldn't have enough to blow his hat off.) The army assassinate a general, but the Tsar survives.
- In 1914 Russia joins the First World War against Germany and suffers terrible defeats. Now the Revolutionaries want peace with Germany but the Tsar won't give in. In fact he says that he'll lead the army himself. So, when it is defeated yet again, the Tsar gets the blame. This time he doesn't survive.

- In March 1917 the Tsar gives up the throne and parliament runs the country and the war. But *that's* not the *real* Russian Revolution. A group of communists calling themselves the Bolsheviks, led by Trotsky and Lenin, *still* want peace and tell the soldiers to disobey parliament. The people are starving – 'The Bolsheviks have to be better than this!' they think.
- In November 1917 the Bolsheviks take over Russia. The Communist Revolution has put the Bolsheviks in power, but of course they just have to spoil the party by squabbling amongst themselves. Millions will die ... including many of the leaders themselves ... in the next 80 years.

Take Trotsky, for example. He lost a struggle for power with the new Russian leader Josef Stalin. Leon knew his old friend Joe would have him killed, so he ran off to hide in Mexico.

Joe Stalin's Secret Police were on his tail and one by one his friends and family were murdered. Leon turned his Mexican house into a fortress and survived another 12 years. On 20 August 1940 he had a young visitor – his last visitor – Ramon Mercader.

Trotsky was heavily guarded. So how did his bodyguard explain what happened next? The guard's statement may have looked something like this...

Date: 21 August 1940
From: Mexican City Police

Call me stupid, but I don't know why you're blaming me. I am innocent, I tell you. I wouldn't harm a hair on Mr Trotsky's head. The old bloke was a genius and a really nice feller. I've been a follower of his sort of communism for years. You can imagine how excited I was when he came to live in Mexico! And when he gave me a job in his household I was thrilled.

'I trust you, Fernando,' he said and his little eyes sparkled behind those glasses. 'I have enemies.'

'The Russian Secret Police,' I said. Even I knew that. 'But this house is like a fortress,' I laughed. 'If anyone gets past the police squad outside they'll have to climb the high concrete walls. And if they try to climb the walls we'll just shoot them down from the machine-gun towers. And even if they do get over you have your bodyguards inside the house. There's not a force in Mexico strong enough to get past these walls, Mr Trotsky.' And I laughed at the very thought.

But the old man was serious. He looked at me over the top of his glasses and said, 'It wouldn't take force to get past the walls. It would take brains.'

Now call me stupid, but I didn't understand what he meant till May this year. The Russian plan was so simple it was brilliant, Mr Trotsky said. The assassins just dressed up as policemen, and walked up to the door. That American Robert Harte went to answer it and they waved a gun in his face. 'Run!' I shouted. 'Leave the door locked, warn Mr Trotsky and hide him!'

So what did Mr Harte do? He opened the door. Of course the Russians marched through the house and sprayed the old man's room with a thousand machine-gun bullets. If Mr Trotsky and his wife hadn't been hiding under the bed they'd have killed him. Of course that Mr Harte went off with the gunmen. He looked quite happy too. Call me stupid, but I reckon he was a spy.

cunning disguise

Policeman's Uniform

Big gun

149

Of course Mr Harte wouldn't have looked too happy when the Russians put a couple of bullets through the back of his head. I hear they found his body a few weeks later. Ruthless those killers were. Ruthless. But it taught us a lesson. It made us much more careful.

'They will try again!' Mr Trotsky told me.

'Better buy a bulletproof bed to be on the safe side,' I laughed. That was a joke, of course, but Mr Trotsky didn't laugh.

Then that Mr Jacson turned up. Lovely young feller and ever so keen. Call me stupid, but I never thought it was suspicious that he wore an overcoat in Mexico in August. Anyway, Mr Trotsky trusted him, so why shouldn't I?

Mr Jacson came back yesterday to show Mr Trotsky some article he'd been writing. 'Mr Trotsky's feeding his rabbits in the garden,' I said. Very tasty those rabbits when they're grown. But that's not the point, is it?

I saw Mr Jacson had his overcoat over his arm, but I never thought that was suspicious, did I? I showed him into Mr Trotsky's office and called the old man in from the garden. Then I left them together.

OVERCOAT

?

The next thing I hear is this terrible scream. I rush to the door and there's Mr Trotsky with one of those ice-pick things sunk right into his skull and blood trickling down the back. Ruined his shirt collar it did. Still he managed to speak.
'Don't kill him – make him talk!'

The police came running in from outside and I passed on Mr Trotsky's message. Mr Jacson had a dirty great knife and a gun hidden in that coat and they reckon he planned to kill himself after he killed Mr Trotsky. I wonder if he planned to shoot himself then stab himself or stab himself then shoot himself?

Yes, I know I was supposed to search people and I know I should have spotted an ice-pick, a dagger and a gun in the coat pockets, but Mr Jacson seemed such a friendly man. Now they tell me poor old Mr Trotsky died today. Oh, dear, I guess you could call me a bit of a failure. And I know you will call me stupid – but please don't call me an assassin.

Fernando

Jacson turned out to be a Spaniard called Ramon Mercader. He was found guilty of murder and sentenced to 20 years in prison which he survived and he was eventually set free.

Joe Stalin said, 'The killing of Trotsky had nothing to do with me!' Yet, back in Russia, Jacson-Mercader was given 'The Order of Lenin', their highest award, so it looks like Joe was telling porkies.

Rotten Romania

Secret police don't just seek out human traitors. They will seek and destroy feathered friends too!

The Romanian Communist leader from 1965 till 1989, Nicolae Ceausescu, had a son called Nicu. The Romanian secret police heard about a parrot that had been taught to say 'Stupid Nicu!' The parrot was arrested and taken to police headquarters where it was questioned. It refused to squawk the answer to the key question: 'Who taught you to say that?' This tough old bird was silenced for good when the secret police twisted its neck.

Hot shots

After thousands of years of revolution you'd think the human race would settle down and learn to live peacefully. But, instead of getting better, the 20th century saw things get worse. New weapons meant that revolutionaries could kill more government forces and government forces could massacre more revolutionaries.

An example of improving weapons can be seen in the execution of old leaders or revolutionaries.

In 1871 the Archbishop of Paris was stood up against a wall and shot by a firing squad. After the smoke cleared the Archbishop was bleeding but still standing. A teenage member of the firing squad called out, 'In the name of God, he must be wearing armour!' He wasn't. The soldiers were simply rotten shots with poor weapons.

A hundred and eighteen years later the Romanian dictator, Nicolae Ceausescu, was sat on a chair to face a firing squad. The firing squad used a machine-gun. The victim didn't suffer as much, the firing squad didn't miss.

That's what's called 'progress'.

Of course one day people may stop butchering one another altogether. That's what's called 'real progress' ... but that will probably take more than another couple of hundred years to be seen.

How to be revolting

Get a slogan, get a song

All the best rebels have a song and a slogan. A little phrase that they can shout as they murder their enemies. The song helps them march into battle and the slogan means they don't have to think.

Rotten revolutionary rule: the shorter your slogan the better. Let's face it, you can't have a slogan that proclaims...

WE THE PEOPLE OF FREEDONIA WANT TO PASS OUR OWN LAWS THAT WILL LET US WORK ONE DAY A WEEK AND HAVE SIX SATURDAYS. WE ALSO WANT DEATH TO ALL TYRANTS, TEACHERS AND TRAFFIC WARDENS, THE BURNING DOWN OF PUBLIC SCHOOLS AND FREE ICE CREAM FOR BREAKFAST EVERY DAY

You'd run out of breath if you tried to chant it, and if you painted that lot on a banner your arms would get tired before you'd murdered your first tyrant.

Here are some of the world's best...

Savage slogans
1 *'Death before slavery'* – *slogan of Jewish defenders of Masada fortress, AD 73*
There were just seven survivors of the siege of Masada in south-east Israel – five children and two women. The other 960 men, women and children cried, 'Death before slavery' ... and then died to prove they believed it.

The historian Josephus Flavius talked to the survivors and described what happened. We can imagine the story of one of the children...

Oh, dear! I suppose you'll burn me alive or throw me to the lions now, won't you? That's what you Romans have been doing to us Jews, isn't it? That's why we shut ourselves into this fortress at Masada. My mum said she didn't want to be a human candle or a lion's lunch.

I remember my dad telling us all about you Romans three years ago. He said your General Titus captured Jerusalem and sent the Jews to the arena in Rome to die. That's why we came here to Masada. 'They'll never get in here!' he said. 'King Herod built this place 40 years ago and it's the greatest fortress in the world!'

We thought it was funny when you camped on the plains below. 'They'll never climb up here!' we laughed. Then General Titus started building a wall all the way around Masada. 'What's he doing that for, Dad?' I asked.

'Making sure we can't escape,' Dad said grimly. 'He wants to take us alive so he can torture us.'

'We don't want to escape, Dad,' I said. 'We're safe in here. He'll never get in, will he?'

'Never,' Dad said.

Then you Romans started building a great ramp out of earth and stones. After a year it was right up to the walls. You charged up the ramp and smashed down the walls. We tried to barricade the gap with wood but you burned it down last night. We knew you were waiting for daylight. We knew you would come in to get us this morning.

There was a big meeting last night. Our leader Eleazar ben Yair said, 'Death before slavery!' and everyone cheered.

Except my dad said, 'How can we *all* die?'

And that's when Eleazar came up with his plan. The men drew lots and Eleazar chose the ten who would kill the other 950 of us.

The ten who were left would be killed by one and then he would kill himself. What happened to us? Well, my mum saw the families lying down and getting the chop, one after another and she said, 'I'm not having those nasty men cut your heads off, my babies. We'll just go off and hide in a drain.'

And that's what we did. The last executioner paddled through all the blood, finished off any that were still alive, found his family and fell on his sword. He made it just in time before you lot broke in. 'Death before slavery!' he cried. Then he sort of said, 'Ouch!' when he fell on his sword.

> My mum says it should be 'Slavery before death!'
> So what's going to happen to me? And what if the lion isn't hungry? Will it still eat me?

We don't know what happened to the seven survivors of the Masada suicide pact.

Don't feel too sorry for the men who died at Masada. They were members of a fanatical group known as the 'Zealots'. When the revolt against the Romans started in AD 54 the Zealots turned to terrorism and assassination and became known as 'Sicarii' (from the Greek word meaning 'dagger men'). They roamed through public places with hidden daggers to strike down people who were friendly to Rome.

Imagine your dad walking around your local supermarket and being stabbed just because he voted Conservative at the last election!

In 1965 the fortress at Masada was excavated by archaeologists and they found pieces of pottery with Jewish names scratched on them. These could have been the names drawn out of the hat to decide who would do the killing. Creepy.

2 *'When Adam delved and Eve span, who was then the gentleman?' – slogan of English Peasants' Revolt, 1381*
Not a very catchy slogan but good for chanting as you march on London, burning houses and cutting heads off lords.

What does it mean, you ask? It means that when God created Adam to delve (dig), and Eve to spin, there were no lords (gentlemen) to boss us humans around. In short ... 'Lords? Who needs them?'

In fact this slogan was an old proverb that the rebel priests used to preach to the peasants in 1381.

3 *'No taxation without representation'* – *18th-century American Revolution*

The British ruled North America and taxed the people there. But the Americans weren't represented in Britain's parliament. So they refused to pay the taxes unless they were represented. As a slogan this is a bit of a failure. You can't chant it, sing it or march to it … you can hardly *say* it! But the revolution was quite a success! Which just goes to show, it's the thought that counts.

4 *'Liberty, equality, fraternity'* – *18th-century French Revolution*

That's better – especially in French. You could march along chanting 'Liberté, egalité, fraternité!' – freedom, equality, fraternity – as you dodged the blood that splashed down from the severed heads on the guillotine. Of course the French peasants weren't *free*, and they certainly weren't *equal* – after the revolution they were poorer than ever. Fraternity means 'brotherhood', of course, and the Bible said the world's first murder victim was killed by his brother!

5 *'Fire and blood'* – *20th-century South American revolutions, Ché Guevara*
'If mankind is ever to escape from its misery,' Ché said, 'there is only one method: the destruction of everything in fire and blood … there is no other way, no other hope.'

But the fire that finished him off was gunfire. And the blood was leaking out of the ends of his arms when his hands were cut off as proof that he'd been killed.

This slogan should really be *'Other people on* fire and *other people's* blood.'

6 *'They shall not pass'* – *slogan of Spanish Republican rebels in Spanish Civil War, 1937*
Great slogan! Still used today by wrinkly drivers of Morris Minor cars on narrow country roads when holding up a ten-mile queue of traffic.

Also used by despairing teachers of GCSE exam pupils in some secondary schools.

'They shall not pass' was the battle cry invented by Dolores Ibarruri when her Republicans were fighting against the Spanish Government forces. Dolores ('Dolly' to you and me, but Ibarruri to the rest of the world) was defeated in the revolution. Maybe she could have changed her slogan to an even shorter one…

Dolly also came up with a second cracking slogan…

It is better to die on your feet than to live on your knees.

159

But, when Dolly's Republicans were crushed she didn't die on her feet. She used her feet to carry her off to the safety of Russia. (Oh, all right then, she used her feet to carry her to the aeroplane that *flew* her off to Russia if you want to be picky.)

Dolly's Spanish enemy, General Franco, finally died of old age, nearly 40 years later. She returned to Spain, a heroine, before dying in 1989.

7 *'Death to the Hats!'* – *slogan of the workers in Florence, 1378*
The workers of Florence were fed up with the posh people who ruled them. They nicknamed the noblemen 'the Hats' and the workers called themselves 'the Cloaks'.

The Hats were really snobbish and when the workers went on strike they sneered, 'Get back to your cloth-making' and 'Go back and grind your pepper.'

Let's face it, *you* would get upset if someone told you to go and grind *your* pepper.

One of the most important of the Hats (you could call him a Top Hat) said...

> *The workers are robbers and traitors, murderers and assassins, gluttons and law-breakers!*

He should have added 'arsonists' because the workers grew so angry they started burning the houses of the Hats, forced their way into the palace and took over the city.

8 *'Workers of the world unite! You have nothing to lose but your chains' – written by revolutionary writers Karl Marx and Friedrich Engels, 1848*

No sooner had Karl Marx published these words than revolution broke out in France, Italy, Austria and Germany!

It was another 70 years before Karl's ideas (called Communism) really caught on. This is probably because the workers weren't great readers and his book is very thick. It may have taken them 50 years to get through it and another 20 to understand it. But, it's a great slogan.

Terrible tunes

Of course, if you really want something longer and stronger than a slogan to express your feelings you need a revolutionary song.

Rule 1: It needs a good tune that people can whistle when they forget the words – or an old song that you can fit new words to...

Rule 2: It has to be violent and bloodthirsty. You know the sort of thing.

Top of the revolutionary pops

Here are some stirring, real revolutionary songs. First you have to match the song to the country. Then, to make it difficult, you have to spot the odd one out.

1 *Come you children of the Mother-land, the day of glory has arrived.*
The tyrant has raised his bloody banner against us,
Can't you hear the roar of his cruel soldiers across the country?
They are coming to butcher your friends and family.
Citizens, take up arms, form your regiments and march.
Wash the fields with their evil blood!

162

2 *Come here in sorrow and you'll be made well;*
   You can escape from the burning of Hell.
   Satan's a devil, a terrible sight,
   Who will dip you in tar and then set you alight.

3 *Running with a dream*
   Burning deep inside,
   Don't let them bring you down,
   Don't let this chance go by.

4 *Their blood has washed out their foul footstep's*
   pollution.
   No refuge could save the hireling and slave
   From the terror of flight
   Or the gloom of the grave

5 *Eia, Eia, Alala!*

163

Answers: **1e)** Cheerful stuff, written one night in 1792 during the French Revolution. But, did you know, this song is now the French national anthem? They sing it before sporting events to encourage French teams to 'wash the field with the blood of the opposition'. (This is clearly unfair. Blood-soaked pitches are very slippery and it's terrible trying to get bloodstains out of your soccer shorts or netball knickers.)

2d) This was a song of the Flagellants. In 1349–50 they marched through Europe whipping themselves because they believed their suffering would drive away the devil who had brought the Black Death. In fact they probably helped to spread the plague! The Catholic Church hated the Flagellants and the Flagellants turned to revolution against the priests. Stoning priests to death was a favourite trick of theirs. Then the Church fought back and Flagellant leaders were burned alive while followers were hanged. The remaining rebel Flagellants simply went home. End of revolution.

3a) This stirring German song was written for the football World Cup of 1998. So of course it's the odd one out.

4b) This is part of the national anthem, *The Star-Spangled Banner*. It was written by a US lawyer after he watched a British defeat during the 1812 war. 'Their blood' refers to the British that the American rebels had driven out. The 'hireling and slave' who either 'fled in terror' or ended up in the 'gloom of the grave' were the British soldiers. Nowadays the Brits and Yanks are great buddies … so the Americans don't sing the verse with these words. (For fear they might upset their friends whose 'foul footsteps' are finally forgiven.)

5c) Italian rebels marched around chanting this in 1919. Their leader, the poet D'Annunzio, said these were the words used by the ancient Greek hero, Achilles, to drive his horses forward. Of course Achilles was just a character from Greek legend so he never shouted anything, let alone: 'Eia, Eia, Alala!'

Did you know…?

The national anthem of the United Kingdom was written to encourage people to resist a revolution. In 1745 Bonnie Prince Charlie landed in Scotland and declared that his father was King James of Scotland and England. Charlie gathered his Highland army and marched towards England. The English people rallied round a new song, *God Save our King,* and that is still the national anthem today.

DON'T PANIC CHAPS! OUR BOFFINS HAVE BEEN WORKING ON A SECRET WEAPON TO DEFEAT THE REBELS, AND THEY'VE COME UP WITH THIS CHEERY SONG!

But, did you also know … the song now begins 'God save our gracious King (or Queen)'. But when it was first sung it began, 'God save great George our King'.

Just as well he wasn't 'Elizabeth our Queen' or 'Victoria our Empress' because those words just wouldn't fit the tune!

Get a leader

Have you ever seen infants play football? They all run after the ball together. If headless chickens could play football then that's how they would play. They need someone to organize them. A 'manager' off the field to make the plan, and a 'captain' on the field to make sure it is carried out.

Revolutions are like that. If you are going to beat somebody then it helps if you are organized. You need a manager and you need a captain – a planner and a leader. Sometimes the planner and the leader are the same person (a sort of player-manager), but that's risky. If the player-manager is injured then the team is left without a leader.

How do you pick your leaders?

You could start by finding someone with a good name! Let's face it, you'd rather follow a Spartacus into battle than a Mickey Mouse.

So if you have a leader with a naff name then make sure they change it!

The name game

On the right are the names of leaders who had thousands of loyal followers. On the left are the names they had before they changed them. All you have to do is match the new names to the old.

OLD NAME	NEW NAME
1 ERNIE	a) COUNT DRACULA
2 SCHICKLGRUBER	b) BULGAROCTONUS
3 VLAD	c) BLACK GEORGE
4 JUDAS	d) ADOLF HITLER
5 ABU'L-ABBAS	e) THE HAMMERER
6 BASIL	f) CHÉ GUEVARA
7 KARADJORD	g) THE MAD PRIEST
8 JOHN BALL	h) SHEDDER OF BLOOD

Answers: **1f)** Ché Guevara was christened Ernesto – that's 'Ernie' to us horrible historians. In his native country Argentina the people had a peculiar speech habit – they'd often say 'Hey!' in a sentence. You know the sort of thing!

'Hey! How you doing!'

'Hey, I'm all right. But, hey, I'm busy.'

'What you doing, hey?'

'Hey, I'm harvesting.'

'Hey, really? What you harvesting, hey?'

'Hay!'

'Yeah … but what you harvesting, hey?'

'Hey! That's right!'

'I'm asking you what you're harvesting, hey?'

'Yes, I am!'

'Hey?'

'Hay!!!'

…and so on.

Now, in Argentina they pronounced this word 'Ché'. When Ernie went to Cuba they were amused by his use of the word and it became his nickname. Ernie Guevara became Ché Guevara. This is a bit like calling somebody 'Oi!' or 'Huh!' or 'Pffff!' because they use those exclamations. What would *you* be called, hey?

2d) Adolf Hitler's father was called Schicklgruber, though he'd changed it to 'Hitler' before Adolf was born. When Hitler's enemies wanted to make fun of him they called him Schicklgruber. Hitler himself admitted that he'd never have been taken seriously and become Nazi leader if he'd been stuck with his father's name. Considering the misery Mr Hitler brought to the world it's a pity his father didn't schtick with the name.

3a) The Turkish army invaded Transylvania in 1462 but reckoned without the Transylvanian Prince, Vlad Tepes. The prince led the rebellion against the invaders. This Vlad had a charming habit of capturing Turks alive, pushing a sharpened stake through their bodies and standing them by the roadside to die. Twenty thousand bodies stretched for a mile in front of the invaders while crows pecked at the corpses. The fierce Turk invader, Mehmed, was so shocked he called off the invasion and ordered a deep ditch to be dug around his camp to keep out Vlad. Vlad became known as 'the Impaler' and 'Dracula' ... the Dragon. He didn't flit around in the shape of a bat and he didn't suck blood from innocent travellers' necks. But his Dracula name lives on as a monstrous vampire. Would 'Vlad' sound as good?

4e) In 165 BC the Syrians ruled the Jews in Jerusalem. Then a Jewish leader called Judas rose to lead them in rebellion. He was given the name 'Maccabeus' – a Hebrew name which means 'Hammerer'. The Jews were angered by the Syrian attempts to use their temple as a place to worship Greek gods. When the Syrians sacrificed a pig in the temple the Jews were furious (and the pig's family weren't too happy either because they failed to save his bacon). Anyway, the Hammerer hammered the Syrians. (Horrible histories health warning: If you try this in your local temple be careful you don't hammer your thumb because it can be very painful.)

169

5h) In AD 750 Abu'l-abbas led a revolution in Mesopotamia and killed the royal family, the Umayyads. His followers gave him the name al-Saffah, which means 'Shedder of Blood'. But he then went on to dig up old, long-dead Umayyad rulers and had the corpses taken to the market-place. There they were flogged. Maybe they should have called him the 'Shredder of Old Bones'.

6b) The Emperor of Byzantium was ruthlessly dethroned by his own nephew, Basil. But Basil's cruellest acts were still to come. He was determined to conquer his neighbour, Bulgaria, and began by giving the Bulgarian lords honours and lordly titles. When they betrayed him Basil became brutal and bloody towards the Bulgarians. He defeated the Bulgarian army in the year 1014 and took most of their soldiers alive.

Then he gave the gory order…

Bulgarian ruler, Tsar Samuel, took one look at his eyeless army and dropped dead with the shock.

Basil was given the name Bulgaroctonus. This is not some type of fierce dinosaur – it is a Greek word meaning 'slayer of the Bulgars' which is neater than 'eye-putter-outer of the Bulgars'.

7c) Black George was named that because he had dark hair and eyes. As a boy he herded pigs in Serbia and went on to lead the Serbians to freedom from their Turkish conquerors.

But a rival Serbian leader had Black George killed in his sleep. Then he had the dark head cut off, bundled up and sent to the Sultan of Turkey as a present.

It was a black night for George.

8g) John Ball was a leader of the 1381 English Peasants' Revolt and he was known as 'The Mad Priest of Kent' ... though he wasn't a priest (he was thrown out of the Church) and he worked in Yorkshire and Essex then died in Hertfordshire!

Ball was executed in St Albans when the Revolt failed.

Follow that name

Here are some odd names that some rebels didn't change ... except for one. Which one is false?

1 Prokop the Bald – Bohemian rebel, 1420s

2 Sauce the Grocer – French revolutionary, 1790s

3 Krum the Khan – Bulgarian leader, 810

4 Bogomil the Priest – Religious leader, 940s

5 Joaquim the Dentist – Brazilian freedom-fighter, 1780s

6 Gut-Ache – Zulu rebel chief, 1820s

7 Rain in the Face – Native American Indian rebel, 1870s

8 Passion Flower – Spanish revolutionary, 1937

Answers: All true except for 8: **1** True. Prokop the Bald was his nickname, Prokop the Slaphead was probably the name his enemies gave him.

2 True. When the French Revolution started, the King and Queen tried to run away. Monsieur Sauce, a local grocer and magistrate, held the runaways and sent them back to Paris for the chop. Chops are better with Sauce.

3 True. Krum led the Bulgars against the mighty Byzantine invaders. He killed the enemy Emperor Nicephorus I and had his skull lined with silver. Then Krum used the skull as a drinking cup – which is a krummy sort of thing to do.

4 True. Bogomil said God made heaven but the Devil made everything on the Earth. His peasant followers, the Bogomils, were persecuted by the Christian Church because they won't do as they're told. Do you know school pupils like that? Then you can call them a Bogomil!

5 True. Joaquim da Silva was a leader in the fight to free Brazil from her Portuguese rulers. But he was an expert dentist and his nickname became 'Tiradentes' (Tooth-puller). He was the only rebel in that revolution to be executed. The Dentist was hanged and cut into pieces as an example to others. There are still lots of people who would love to see their dentist cut into pieces!

PS Please note: No jokes about Joachim the Dentist looking 'down in the mouth' at his trial. That joke is too bad even for a Horrible Histories book.

6 True. When Shaka's mother became pregnant she said, 'It's not a baby, it's *ishaka*.' And *ishaka* means a pain in the stomach. When the baby was born he was known as *Shaka*, after his mother's complaint. But Shaka caused more than a gut-ache to many people. He killed his father and took over the leadership of the Zulu nation. Then he was terrified of growing old. He believed that having children aged a man so he murdered any of his wives who gave birth to a child.

When Shaka's mum died he was so upset he ordered hundreds to be slaughtered. Somehow this maniac made the Zulu nation huge and powerful. By 1840 his violence was out of control and most of his people were happy when he was speared to death by his half-brother.

7 True. Rain in the Face was captured by the Seventh Cavalry and escaped. His captor was the younger brother of the famous general Custer – Tom Custer. When Rain in the Face escaped, he swore he would return and eat Tom Custer's heart!

At the Battle of the Little Big Horn, Rain in the Face finally met up with Tom Custer again … and kept his promise to eat the soldier's heart.

8 False. It wasn't her *real* name. Dolores Ibarruri wrote rebel articles in newspapers and called herself by the pen-name 'La Pasionaria'. This Spanish word, meaning 'Passion Flower', became the name she was often known by.

Compared to 'The Black Hand Gang' a name like 'Passion Flower' doesn't strike terror into your heart, does it?

The potty poet

If you can't find someone with a good name then find someone who *looks* good and who *acts* well.

After the First World War, Italy had the potty poet Gabriele D'Annunzio. (Gabby wrote his poems with a quill pen on the back of an open umbrella and if you think that's not potty you're a pink Pomeranian poodle.)

Gabby had *style*. In the 1914–18 war he fought on land, sea and air.

• **Land** He led a charge on the Austrian trenches, wearing a huge, flapping cloak, carrying a dagger between his teeth and holding a pistol in each hand.

• **Air** He flew over Vienna and dropped red, white, and green leaflets from an aeroplane. The leaflets boasted how kind the Italians were not to be dropping bombs.

• **Sea** He took a small torpedo boat into the Austrian fleet at the Bay of Bucari and sank a much larger warship. He lost an eye in the fighting and won lots of medals.

The fact that he was short, bald, fat and with an ugly, swollen nose didn't matter. He was the sort of rebel hero people like to follow.

But what does a hero do after war is finished? He gets bored. He goes looking for trouble. All he needed was something to fight for.

Gabby found it in the town of Fiume. When peace arrived in 1918 no one was quite sure who should rule Fiume. Gabby decided he should claim it for Italy ... even though the Italian government didn't want him to. Gabby made sure that film cameras were there to record his entry into the town. It must have made a wonderful true-drama, all-action entertainment in the cinemas...

HE WAS MET BY ITALIAN GENERAL PITTALUGA, A PITILESS AND POMPOUS MAN WITH A POINTING PISTOL PRIMED

GENERAL: "GO NOW, YOU REBEL RUFFIAN, OR BE SHOT!"
D'ANNUNZIO: "THE AUSTRIANS COULDN'T KILL ME - NOR CAN YOU!"
CROWD: CHEERS!

GO GO GABBY

THE POWERFUL POET PULLED OPEN HIS CLOAK AND CRIED: "THEN ORDER YOUR TROOPS TO SHOOT ME, GENERAL!"

"SHOOT"

BUT THE BRAVE ITALIAN BOYS REFUSED!

THE TROOPS REBELLED AND WENT OVER TO D'ANNUNZIO'S SIDE. THE POET WAS THE UNCROWNED KING OF FIUME.

THE END

Of course it wasn't the end. D'Annunzio was a lousy leader and his followers lived a lawless life for a year. Then the Italian forces moved in and took over once more. Most of the rebels were glad to be united with Italy again.

Still, D'Annunzio was honoured by the new Italian government and gave up being a rebel.

Kwick killer kwiz

Torture your teacher with these curious kwestions about assassins – answer true or false. Add a bit of excitement by telling them they go to the guillotine if they get less than 11 out of ten...

1 A gunman called Zangara shot at US President Franklin D Roosevelt because he blamed the President for the pains in his stomach.

2 In 1981 US President Reagan was shot by John Hinckley because Hinckley wanted the actress Jodie Foster to take notice of him.

3 Queen Victoria was so popular no one ever tried to assassinate her though she reigned over 60 years.

4 US President Lincoln was shot dead even though he was guarded by 20 men.

5 In 1944 a bomb plot to kill Adolf Hitler only succeeded in blowing his trousers off.

6 Charles Guiteau shot President Garfield in 1881. After his execution his skull was put on display in the Washington Medical Museum where it can be seen today.

7 Indira Gandhi, Prime Minister of India, was shot by the men who were given the job of protecting her.

8 In 1835 a Corsican attacked King Louis Philippe of France and shot at him with 25 guns.

9 In 1835 a crazed gunman fired two pistols at US President Jackson and both pistols misfired. Yet the President had a bullet in his body.

10 As Caesar was stabbed to death in 44 BC he pulled his toga over his face so he couldn't see the knives.

Answers: **1** True. Zangara went to a meeting, stood up on a chair to get a better view, took aim and fired. He missed the President but killed the mayor who was sitting on the same platform. Zangara was sentenced to die in the electric chair, which must have come as a bit of a shock.

2 True. President Reagan survived the stomach wound though his bodyguard was badly injured. The President had been a movie star himself but the bullets in those western films never hurt as much as Hinckley's. Hinckley admitted he was mad and avoided going to trial. He was probably mad at failing to catch Jodie Foster's eye.

3 False. There were about eight attempts on Victoria's life. They all failed, the attackers were usually caught and found to be mad. Victoria wanted them all to be executed – in fact, the attackers were mostly given short prison sentences. Victoria was not amused.

4 False. President Lincoln was guarded by one policeman who sat outside the door to the President's gallery at the theatre. The man got bored and went off for a drink. The assassin simply walked in, placed a pistol to Lincoln's head and pulled the trigger. Policeman drinkin' let assassin slink in and no more thinkin' for Lincoln.

5 True ... sort of. In July 1944 a bomb in a briefcase was placed under the table where Adolf Hitler was holding a meeting. By chance an officer moved the briefcase behind the leg of the heavy table. When it exploded it killed several people but the leg saved Hitler's life. He was deafened and suffered a numb arm and burns to his face ... but he lived. The greatest damage was to his trousers that were practically blown away and turned his famous moustache t' ash.

6 False. Guiteau did assassinate Garfield and his executed body was sent to surgeons to cut up for practice. The skull was put on display in Washington Medical Museum ... but it's not there now. Somebody pinched it and it has never been recovered! Many failed rebels have lost their head – but it must be rare for a government to lose a rebel's head for him!

7 True. Bodyguards make great assassins because they are in the best place to kill their victim. Mrs Gandhi's bodyguards were given the job of escorting her to a television interview, and they knew she wouldn't be wearing her bullet-proof vest in front of the cameras. After they filled her full of bullets they laid down their guns and raised their hands to surrender ... but no one came to arrest them. When the other guards heard the shooting they ran away and hid! Mrs Gandhi's father had been assassinated by gunmen too and when her son took over from her he did wear a bullet-proof vest – but it didn't help Rajiv when a woman walked up to him to present him with flowers. There was a bomb strapped to her body and she activated it to kill him and kill herself … not to mention 14 innocent people. Three of the Gandhi family died at the hands of assassins yet the Congress Party tried to persuade Rajiv's wife, Sonia Gandhi, to stand for parliament. Would you? Sonia Gandhi didn't.

8 True. Guiseppe Fiesci rigged up a machine to fire 25 guns all at once. As King Louis Philippe went to inspect his troops Fiesci fired the world's first machine-gun and killed 18 people. But he missed his target, the King! Fiesci went to the guillotine; it didn't take 25 chops to kill him and the executioner didn't miss. As his head fell into the basket, Fiesci's last thought must have been…

9 True. When President Jackson was elected he had *two* bullets in his body. The first was left in his arm after a gun fight 20 years before. It was removed shortly after he became President. Then Jackson got himself into a duel over a gambling debt. His rival's bullet hit close to his heart and stayed there. (Jackson shot the other man in the groin and killed him.) That second bullet was still there when the gunman shot at him in 1835. This was the first ever attempt to assassinate an American president where the assassin was the heir to the British throne! At least that's who the gunman *said* he was – other people said he was a house painter called Richard Lawrence and he was as potty as his paint pots.

10 False. Caesar let the top of his toga drop so it covered his legs. He didn't want to die with his legs showing. If the killers had had their way he'd have been showing more than his legs. They planned to strip him and throw his body in the river. But as he lay there dead they were horrified by what they'd done and they ran away. Three common slaves carried Caesar home instead.

Did you know…?

The ruler of Morocco had once rebelled against the Caliph of Baghdad and lost. The Caliph waited five years for his revenge and got it in an unusual way. In AD 791 he sent his enemy a poisoned toothpick which killed him as soon as he put it into his mouth.

Wonder what they put on his gravestone? 'He took his pick'?

Staying alive

Leaders can become very nervous and do some strange things to stay alive.

Nicolae Ceausescu – Romania

The Romanian dictator from 1965 till 1989 was scared of being assassinated by revolutionaries. He deserved it. So Nicolae…

- disinfected his hands every time he'd shaken hands with a foreign leader – including Queen Elizabeth II of Britain – in case the hand passed on germs or poison

- used a food taster before he would eat anything, even at royal or state banquets

- held meetings in the middle of gardens because he was sure every room he went in was bugged

- wore every item of clothing only once because he'd heard of plots to poison a leader's clothes

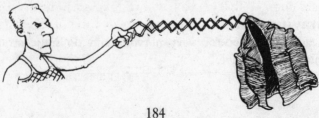

• made his wife take her own bed and towels with her everywhere – even to Buckingham Palace

• gave his black Labrador dog its own bedroom with television and telephone; to protect it the dog even had its own doctor to taste its food.

All of these wonderful schemes seem to have worked and Nicolae Ceausescu was never poisoned. Of course they were not much help when the revolutionaries tied him to a chair and put him in front of a firing squad. A bullet-proof vest may have been better protection than disinfectant soap.

King Kon's canine

Nicolae Ceausescu wasn't the only ruler devoted to his dog. In 1920 King Konstantinos had only one friend in Greece – his pet dog. So, when the dog was attacked by monkeys, the King rushed to his rescue. (You've heard of guard dogs? Well, King Kon was a dog guard.) The monkeys bit the King, the wound became infected and the King died in agony from blood poisoning. You'll be thrilled to know the dog survived.

This is the only recorded case of an assassinating ape.

Epilogue

Would you like to be part of a revolution? Millions of people have fought – or simply been caught – in the violence and millions have died.

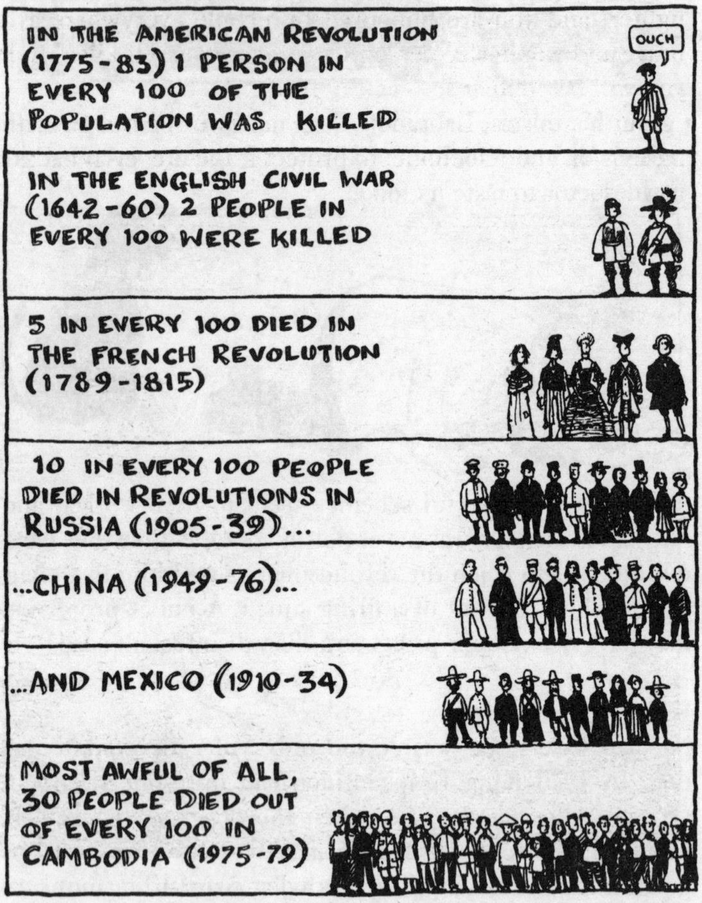

IN THE AMERICAN REVOLUTION (1775 - 83) 1 PERSON IN EVERY 100 OF THE POPULATION WAS KILLED

OUCH

IN THE ENGLISH CIVIL WAR (1642 - 60) 2 PEOPLE IN EVERY 100 WERE KILLED

5 IN EVERY 100 DIED IN THE FRENCH REVOLUTION (1789 - 1815)

10 IN EVERY 100 PEOPLE DIED IN REVOLUTIONS IN RUSSIA (1905 - 39)...

...CHINA (1949 - 76)...

...AND MEXICO (1910 - 34)

MOST AWFUL OF ALL, 30 PEOPLE DIED OUT OF EVERY 100 IN CAMBODIA (1975 - 79)

You can see that revolutions are getting bloodier as time goes by, as new weapons are produced and people get better at killing each other. At that rate there'll be no one left in revolutions of the future!

So why have so many taken such risk and suffered so much?

Because life was so bad under their rulers that even death was better than suffering. And there's always a chance that you could win!

If you do win then you become famous as a 'freedom fighter' and you are honoured by people everywhere as a brave and wonderful person. If you get yourself killed then you will be popular for ever more.

But if you lose, of course, you are not called a freedom fighter. You are called a 'terrorist' and you are despised as a ruthless assassin.

Revolutions can be bloody, cruel and unfair.

But there are some leaders who are so vicious, violent and insane that *someone* has to stop them. Murderous rulers – like Adolf Hitler of Germany, Josef Stalin of Russia or thousands of others – have to be stopped.

Sometimes they can be stopped by fair means – sometimes they have to be stopped by foul.

By revolution.

In the end it is down to individuals like you. Is it better to live on your knees ... or to die on your feet?

Only you can decide.

AFTERWORD

INTERESTING INDEX